ACTION & IDEA
The Roots of Entertainment

Second Edition

Edward EmanuEl
California State University-Fresno

KENDALL/HUNT PUBLISHING COMPANY
4050 Westmark Drive   Dubuque, Iowa 52002

Contents

Introduction

Entertainment is no longer just something to do with your loose change! Worldwide, it is a trillion dollar industry. It is a business which is both run by international companies such as Gulf-Western and by little mom and pop enterprises such as your local video store.

Most of us get involved with the entertainment industry on a daily basis. We go to the movies, turn on TV sets, play Nintendo, participate in Jr. soccer league, listen to the radio in your car or probably to a walk-man strapped on your head while you're in this class. All of it is entertainment and all of it is big money . . . your money.

You're a consumer. And as a consumer there is always somebody out there trying to separate you from your hard earned money. Every time you buy a ticket to a movie you become part of the American way of life: spend money on products. However, where the Federal Government protects most consumers from being stuck with faulty products, the Feds have no such lemon laws to protect you from a boring movie! Just try and get your money back after you've been fooled into going to a bad film! Just try and get your electric company to knock a couple of bucks from your next bill because you saw some terrible TV. Try to get your pay-per-view bucks back after a boring boxing match. So, the only way to protect yourself is to educate yourself. You don't have to be a victim! You can fight back! You and only you can improve the quality of entertainment. Producers produce for consumption so if you demand a better product then you will get it!

Disney knew that *The Lion King* and *Alladin* would rake in the big bucks. *Beevis and Butthead* rake in big bucks too. The question is this: what do two great entertaining films have to do with two brainless MTV hustlers? They are closer than you think! This book will tell you why.

When you go to a football game and you scream and yell when your team scores a touchdown, then you are watching one of the oldest forms of entertainment in the history of the world: athletics. Is there any relationship between a fifty yard pass reception for a touchdown and *Rocky* (one through twenty-five!)? You bet.

In fact, there is very little in this world that doesn't fall into the category of entertainment. All you have to do is understand the basic elements of entertainment and then you will begin to become an expert on boredom and how to relieve it. And once you understand how entertainment works then you will understand when you're being hustled out of your money. Once you understand and recognize the essence of what is entertainment and what is not then you will be in a great position for the consumer to tell the producer what to do. And afterall, if knowledge is power, then getting power over the entertainment producers will make you, the consumer, a force to be reckoned with and listened to. Be smart! Don't let the producers tell you how to spend your money. Get educated and then you will get better entertainment.

Theater and Drama
Are All Around Us

It's all around us. It never stops. There's no intermission and most of the time it's free. The "it" is entertainment. If you're ever bored then you must be either stupid or unaware. For the sake of making an enemy out of you let's just assume you're just unaware how entertaining everything around you is. When you were kids it was easy to let your imaginations run free. The world was pretty magical. Then somehow you grew up and suddenly all of that magic turned into reality. Reality is boring. But the secret here is that nothing changed except you. The world is still magical but you aren't. But getting the magic back isn't difficult. It just requires you to use your imagination instead of your ego. Your ego is your worst enemy. It keeps you from enjoying life to its fullest because it is always protecting you from making a "fool" out of yourself. The truth is that there is no such thing as being foolish or nerdy or dweeb-like or any of the other derisive descriptions identifying unacceptable behavior as defined by the boring masses. There is only theatrical and dramatic behavior or non-theatrical and non-dramatic behavior.

Learning how to view the world, indeed the universe, as a giant movie screen waiting to amaze and delight you is the key to keep you from being bored. For the purpose of categorizing let us divide entertainment into two concepts: Theatre and Drama.

Theatre is defined as, "how the world is perceived by our emotion." Theatre appeals to our emotions and our five senses. Anything that stimulates our emotions falls into the category of theatre. Drama, on the other hand, is defined as, "what is perceived by our brains." Anything that requires thought, understanding, analysis, synthesis, or mind perception is drama. Words fall into the world of drama because words must be translated through our brains. But actions fall into the world of theatre because they stimulate the emotions. Obviously, drama requires more energy to deal with than theatre. Drama deals with morals, proverbs, ideas, and attitudes. Here is an example:

You pick up a newspaper and the headline says, "Famous sports figure dies while playing golf." The drama is death. That's clear. But how did the sports figure die? The answer to that question will be the theatre of the event. Let's say the sportsman was struck by lightning and blew up in a spectacular burst of light . . . now that's an example of theatre! So, "what" happened on the golf links? Death. "How" did it happen? Spectacularly. Theatre is how something happened and Drama is what happened.

Theatre is made up of seven elements: 1) Violence 2) Sex 3) Anticipation 4) Fear 5) Spectacle 6) Music and 7) Laughter. These elements of theatre can be found in most successful entertainments. Certainly movies have most of these elements and normally sporting events contain at least violence, anticipation, and perhaps fear. Rock concerts stir the passions so much that sometimes the audience becomes part of the theatrical event! Even less obvious theatre events can become exciting if you realize that an element of theatre is taking place. For example, rain becomes an element of theatre if it changes the way you feel about the weather. Notice the operative word here is, "feel." Does graffiti make you angry? If you get angry then you are experiencing a theatrical event. If you ask yourself, "Why would anybody want to mark up peoples' walls? then you are experiencing a dramatic event. And if you examine your own neighborhood you might be surprised to see a theatrical event and a dramatic event taking place every second! Actually, this is how a film is made. The writer notices all of the elements of theatre taking place in real life and then artistically selects the events that fit into a good story (the story is the drama) and the film is written! The trick is in the selection of those elements of theatre which attract an audience.

The number one element of theatre is violence. More money is made by showing violence than any other element of theatre. Why? What is there in violence that makes people, especially in America, want to pay to see it?

Anthropologists have given us thousands of books on the nature of evolution and humankind's great technological advances. What most of these scientists fail to discuss with us is the evolution of the soul. I can hear you now, "Come on Dr. EmanuEl, you can't scientifically address that subject!" You're right . . . but through observation we can draw assumptions. First, there is no question that violence is a daily occurrence on the streets of large American cities. Look at any of the TV talk shows and you'll notice that people freely discuss how they beat up their girlfriends and their boyfriends! Compare the level of violence in American movies between the 1940s and the 1990s and you will notice that the modern movies are much more violent. And while all of this is happening we are getting media blitzes begging people not to resort to violence! Churches, temples, and houses of worship from all religions send the message home: "Love thy neighbor." But in fact, we don't love our neighbors! We shoot at our neighbors! Why? Technology has outstripped the evolution of sense of right and wrong. We're only a very short time out of the trees! In terms of the development of our planet, humans have been here a very short time. We are still too close to our primordial roots which suggest that killing is acceptable behavior. Maybe in a million years our souls will catch up to brains. I can hear you again. You're saying, "But Dr. EmanuEl, you're wrong! I am not a violent person. I hate violence and I will not participate in violence." I can prove to you that you are wrong. Let's say that I'm lecturing to you. And without any reason at all I come to you and strike you right across the face and then go on lecturing as if nothing had happened. You would sit there in a state of shock, maybe embarrassment, perhaps in a state of anger, and maybe you will start crying. Suddenly, I return to you and hit you again!

Now there is no question in my mind; you will hate me! You will hope that the next step I take will fling me into a bottomless pit of hell! The senseless violence on my part has inspired you to hate me! You may not stand up and scream at me. You may not rush me and try to hurt me. But there is no question you feel anger even if you keep it bottled up inside of you. And rightly so. You are responding normally for our state of evolution. And I will later be arrested for assault and hopefully be put in jail . . . where I will learn much about violence!

Football! From Pop Warner to the pros, from Canada to Australia to the Wimpy League in England everybody loves football! In the USA it is the most successful sports entertainment that we have. Figured it out? Violence! Twenty-two men don't line up on the field of battle to miss each other! It is a "game" designed to hurt people. The physical description of the game is perfect for lovers of violence. Listen to the words: "Sack" which means to tear down and destroy. "Bump and Run." "Illegal use of the hands." "Crunching tackle." All of it means violence. And the crowds love it. They pay for it! The bigger the men, the harder the physical contact, the more violent the collisions, the more popular the "game" becomes. And there's boxing. Is this a sport? Probably. But is it an entertainment? Definitely! Everybody wants his punches to hurt people. His punches knock out people. And people on TV, and in the movies! Right now, at the time this book is being written we are waiting for Tyson to be freed from jail. When that happens and when he again battles for the heavyweight championship(s), his payday will be roughly 20 million dollars. Violence. Big bucks!

And then there's the chance to combine sports with movies. *Rocky* and all following *Rocky* films collectively have made more money than any other kind of film! Why? We love Rocky. We want to see Rocky win. It makes no difference what color you are, what religion you are, what your race is: we all love Rocky. We love him when Apollo Creed knocks him to pieces! We love him when Mr. T. beats him to a pulp. We love him when he covers himself in the flag and raises his gloved hand! We love his violence. We love his ability to conquer. Think of all of the movies that have made mega-bucks and they all have violence as a root entertainment. *ET* is based in violence. Of course it is. Why is ET scared of the guy with the keys? Because he knows, and rightly so, this guy and his kind want to get him on an examining table and cut him up! *The Lion King,* one the biggest money makes of all time is certainly succeeding with a theme of violence in it. *Alladin, Jaws, Star Wars, Batman, Star Trek, Silence of the Lambs* and on and on. The film makers and sports promoters know that you want violence and that you'll pay for it. So as long as you demand it you'll get it. If someday your soul will catch up to the technology then perhaps you'll reject violence. At that time the market place will respond in kind. Supply and demand . . . there's no other way to look at it.

The second most commercial element of theatre is sex. Sex sells. No question about it. Sex is still the forbidden subject that appeals to our sense of curiosity. We label films

R or X because of sexual situations. I personally can't figure out why we can watch bullets rip through a human body and not consider *it* pornographic but the act of two people making love is pornographic. But that's the way our society is. Sex is naughty and embarrassing and a butcher with an ax hacking up coeds isn't embarrassing at all. But there is more to this sex business than just curiosity. The word *vicarious* comes to mind immediately. I assume you won't go to a dictionary so here is a definition of vicarious: pretending. That's it. When you go to a movie there are times that you are so caught up in the action of the film that you project yourself in it! You begin to feel nervous when the hero is about to be hunted down or really excited when the hero is about to defeat the villain. And when it comes to sex scenes often you will project yourself into the heated passion of the love making! This is why we have movie stars with sex appeal. Sometimes they have no talent at all except to make you feel hot! Think about the best actors and actresses in films. How many of them are smart? Of course there are exceptions . . . not many. Sex, in any way, shape, or form, tries to excite you. You even think, "Are they really making love on the movie screen?" The producers try to excite you by inviting you to participate in some way while you're watching. Of course it can go too far. Ask Peewee Herman about that. You can't act out and pretend to have sex in public without getting arrested. But then again I'm sure the producers don't care what you do as long as you buy tickets to see two sexy people having sex in front of you. Sex is a primal emotion. And of course it is very different and distinct from violence, another primal emotion. In *Conan The Barbarian* Conan is seduced by a witch. During the sex scene that follows the witch tries to rape and kill Conan. Is this sex? No. Rape and sex have nothing to do with each other. Later in the film Conan does have sex and it is all very explicit! No violence, just love and sex. The difference is very apparent.

There can be no doubt that the one movie that has made more money than any other movie is a porno. Because it was never released through a major studio we can never really count the box office. But since it was released to all of the XXX theatres in the world it has made countless millions. It still sells more videos than most films. *Deep Throat.* That's right. No big stars, no fancy sets and costumes, just sex . . . and curiosity. Most people are motivated to buy the video because they are curious. The greatest playwright of all time, William Shakespeare, writes about violence and sex. His most famous plays, *Romeo and Juliet, Hamlet, Othello* , and *A Midsummer Night's Dream* all depend on violence and sex to keep their plots moving. Times have not changed.

Anticipation is the third most important element of theatre and it asks the question, "Will it happen or won't it happen?" Anticipation appeals to our most disgusting nature which is one reason why suspenseful anticipation makes so much money in the entertainment field. For example, why do people watch auto races? If you've ever gone to one you know that it's pretty boring. You can't even tell which car is winning after a couple of hours. But there is one thing that everybody knows can happen . . . a crash! Sure we all expect that one of the cars will make a mistake and crash, burn, explode! Terrible as that is, it is perfectly normal for us to anticipate the worst! Our sense of theatre tells us that when machines push the limit, urged on by human drivers, an accident is possible . . . more than possible! And the payoff is something that even exceeds our anticipation. Here's another example. One year the circus came to town. Not a whole lot of people showed up to the Sunday afternoon show but those who were there got their money's worth. The great Madame Zucchini was working sixty feet above the arena floor . . . without a net! She was working in the high wire on a uni-cycle. The best part of her act was where she did a 360 turn lightning fast! Well, that Sunday afternoon her famous 360 turn missed a degree or two and she fell to her death! She fell sixty feet and hit so hard she was literally squashed! The crowd was shocked! Little kids ran home screaming . . . but excited! The newspaper headlines the next day screamed, "Death at the circus!" All in all it was a very exciting afternoon. But that's not the point of the story. It's what happened the next year that's important. The next year all of the advance tickets were sold in a snap! Everybody was trying to get tickets for the circus! They were even scalping tickets in front of the arena! Why? Everybody anticipated another disaster. Everybody was anticipating death. And of course the circus helped it all out by announcing another act just as dangerous as Madame Zucchini's. And the circus stressed that the new high wire act would not have a net! Anticipation depends on payoffs for its entertainment. If we expect something exciting or violent or sexual will take place and it doesn't we're very disappointed. If the Super Bowl has two great offensive teams and final score is 3 to nothing I can guarantee you the anticipation has a negative payoff. If you get a pay-per-view of a champion boxing match and it's over in 30 seconds you feel cheated! You anticipated twelve rounds of great fighting and all you got was some tomato can taking a dive. On the other hand many times you go to a movie or to a live show and the result is better than you anticipated and you feel great!

The fourth element of theatre is fear. Things that make us afraid are very entertaining. There is no question that the movie industry has tried to scare the living . . . "daylights" out of us for the past eighty years! Vampires, Jasons, Hellraisers, and Freddies have all tried to make us spend our entertainment money on them . . . and we have! Fear, and the fun of fear, is ingrained in us when we are very young. Do you remember the thrill of hide-and-seek? You don't! Too bad. It was fun. And what was fun about it was waiting to be caught! It was so exciting! Do you remember tag? You're being chased. The person coming after you just wants to tag you but you won't let it happen because it means you'll be it! But I think this thrill of being made afraid goes back further than childhood. I think somehow, we still retain the campfire feeling of a million years ago. Out primordial ancestors, gathered around the midnight fire, under a full moon, heard the beastly howl of some great predator and their blood turned to ice at the thought of being trapped, stalked, and hunted down. Thrills! Don't forget the theme parks that create incredible machines to scare you. Roller coasters, ferries wheels, virtual reality rides are all designed to scare you and give you thrills. The only problem with fear is that we get used to it. What scares us on Monday may not scare us again on Friday! If you see any of the old fear movies of the 1930s and '40s you'll just laugh at the attempts to scare us. Poor Bella can't make us run screaming from the room. Jason and his hockey mask can't do it anymore. Freddie and his ill kempt nails don't give us that rush of fear at all anymore. Our threshold constantly rises. The same can be said for violence. We always want more and movie producers are only too glad to keeping trying!

Behind the fifth door is spectacle. Ah, mindless, unredeeming, spellbinding spectacle. Spectacle is anything that delights the eye. Anything that entertains the eye! And movie producers, sport promoters, Las Vegas all know the $ value of spectacle. So here it is. We are sitting in the dark . . . then slowly a huge space ship fills the screen. We consciously push ourselves back in our seats as the Dolby sound crushes our inner ear to powder. Suddenly, we experience several sensations. One of them is fear . . . fear of the unknown . . . fear that there is something out there in space that is more powerful than we are. Then we experience anticipation . . . waiting for what comes next and most of all we experience spectacle . . . our eyes cannot leave the screen. That's what happen when I saw *Star Wars*! George Lucas unleashed spectacle and all that goes with it right on top of our heads . . . and we loved it! Exploding stars, incredible spaceship dogfights, monsters on a spectacular level! Wait a minute . . . think for a minute . . . can you remember the plot of *Jurassic Park*? Maybe you can . . . maybe you can't but no matter what you cannot forget Speilberg's fantastic monsters. They shocked you! They delighted you! They reached out and grabbed you! Spectacle takes the place of good writing, good acting, and good directing. But it always sells!

King Kong was the *Jurassic Park* of early sound movies. Now we have virtual reality rides that depend on nothing but realistic spectacle to glue you to your seats . . . because in fact, you never leave you seats even thought you know that you are moving through space, or down a rollercoaster!

Spectacle can take many forms . . . female forms and male forms. Swarzenegger was spectacle and all by himself in *Conan the Barbarian*. And Julia Roberts can keep our eyes delighted anytime she wants to. What about Godzilla? Forget Godzilla . . . it's just silly spectacle. Ray Harryhousen, the creator of dynamotion, made you think little dolls were the size of the Empire State building . . . He made a lot of spectacle movies where the actors were only second to machines.

We take spectacle for granted. Too bad. It can really relieve your boredom. Look outside and study the sky at night. No, you won't do that . . . too much work. But if you did you would be overwhelmed by the beauty of the universe. It requires very little effort, really. Just stand outside and tilt your head up. Well, maybe you need to get out in the country to do that, if you can still find it. And maybe it isn't a good idea to be out there alone . . . you'll get mugged. So look at the city instead. The constant trail of tail lights, the steady stream of multi-colored cars, the neon lights. It's fun to watch. Las Vegas is wonderful and you can have a great time and never gamble once. Even better go to Paris. I know it's expensive. Save your money, it's worth it. See the Eiffel Tower at night. You'll die. Spectacle. It requires no mind . . . just eyes. It requires no education . . . just eyes. It requires no technical experience . . . just eyes. Open them. Actually look. Actually see. Train yourself to examine the world around you not just pass by it. I guarantee it; you'll be fascinated by it. I'm wasting my breath. You won't do it. You're not brave enough to do it. Too bad!

Music is the sixth element of theatre. Music appeals to our emotions more than any other theatre element. Music has power to make you feel any emotion. Music has the power to make you feel sexy, sleepy, angry, patriotic, disgusted, and deaf. Why do you play the music so loud in your cars? It's because you like to feel it pulsating through your body. That's O.K., Beethoven liked the same feeling . . . of course he went deaf. And so will you. Music takes a lot of entertainment money. CDs, videos, tapes of all kinds. All movies need music. They live and die with great or bad soundtracks. I remember when I first heard the music in *Rocky* . . . it made me want to run . . . it's the only thing that has ever made me want to run! My feet naturally start moving when I hear "Gettin' strong now . . . " How about *Eye of the Tiger*? Gives me chills just thinking about it. *Jaws* . . . if only the swimmer could hear "bump-bump, bumpbumpbump" then he'd get out of the water fast!

You bring your date home to your apartment after a great evening. You fix some drinks . . . maybe a little food . . . you turn down the lights . . . and then . . . you turn on some music. You choose the music carefully; you want seduction music! If everything is perfect and you slip on the wrong CD and some jackass wails, "I don't love you no more, 'cause you're nothing but a whore! . . . " the mood is lost! You might as well take a cold shower and go to bed. Music is so powerful that it transcends language, culture, race, or even the planet. That's right, we beam music into outerspace in hope that someone is going to listen to it. Do you remember *Close Encounters of the Third Kind*? Of course you do. The scientists end up communicating with aliens from outerspace through a few musical notes. The scene is so powerful, so spectacular, so musical that it stands out as one of the greatest moments in movie history. We treat musicians just the way we treat actors, sports heroes, and professors (well maybe not professors) as mini-gods! When the Beatles were at their most popular height John Lennon had the gaul to state that they were more popular than Jesus Christ. Not many kids argued with him. Music does something else for us as well. The next time you watch a movie on your VCR, go ahead and turn down the sound during an action scene. You'll notice that the scene seems pretty boring! Amazing! Music actually intensifies spectacle! So, the ear sends signals to our emotions which also sends signals to our eyes! We are now so used to having music supporting all of the other elements of theatre that we really miss music when it isn't there or is bad! What is the difference between bad music and good music when it comes to being an element of the-atre? If the music stands out by itself as something separate from the spectacle or the vi-olence or the fear then we hate it. For example, we wouldn't like to hear soft romantic music while we're watching a gun fight. (Maybe you would but you'd be wrong!) And during a romantic scene you wouldn't want to hear a military march! You might get a laugh out of that and that leads us to our next and final element of theatre: laughter.

What would Jim Carey do without the theatrical element of laughter? Probably look for a career in retail shoes. We love to laugh. The more we laugh the better we feel. Human beings are the only creatures on earth who laugh . . . who feel the emotional need to laugh. We really don't know much about laughter or why people laugh. We think we know why certain actions or words make people laugh but the field is wide open for re-search. Certain words always make us laugh. If I say to you "boo-boo wabba" I bet you'll laugh. No? Well, my six month old baby roars when I say that. Strange. Laughter changes with age. Things that we laughed at when we are young are no longer funny when we get old. And some people can't understand why others are laughing at certain things. Robin Williams makes a lot of people laugh but others sit there and stare at him as if he's talk-ing a strange language. Some people laugh at a guy slipping on the ice and falling down. Surprise makes people laugh. Some people use laughter as a release of tension. You see a woman walking down a lonely street. It's dark. It's scary. Suddenly there is a dark shad-ow following her. She begins to run. it begins to chase. She is screaming in the night. Finally, she is trapped in an alley! The figure comes toward her. He's holding something in his hand! He raises it up! She blocks her face and screams, "No!" Then suddenly we see the dark figure step into the light with a pizza he was trying to deliver to her. "Sorry lady, I didn't know you didn't want the garlic supreme." We laugh! She laughs. It isn't very funny. But that's not why we laugh. We're relieved she's still alive.

Jim Carey is silly. He's the master of silly comedy. *The Mask* was really silly! *Dumb and Dumber* was really silly. And lots of people like to laugh at silly things. Bill Cosby is still funny because we like him. We love him. He says funny things because they seem so real! The Three Stooges still get laughs on videos through pain! Yeah, we laugh at pain. We thank God we're not the one being poked in the eye so we laugh at the poor idiot poked in the eye. *Married With Children* gets laughs by being offensive and brutal. It dehuman-izes everybody! We laugh at it (I don't) but a lot of people do because it continues to stay on TV and will be with us on re-runs for years. *I Love Lucy* never seems to die! Why? Why do we laugh at Lucy, especially after we've seen the same show for the fifty-first time? Lucy gets into stupid situations which require stupid solutions. We laugh at stupid things. *Taxi* was funny because it put unusual people into unusual situations. We laugh at Louie trying to be a lover! We laugh at Latka speaking English! We laugh at Reverend Jim try-ing to be sober. And of course we laugh at ourselves. When we recognize our own silly be-havior in others we find it funny. Laughing is such a emotional release that we tend to forgive entertainments which aren't very good if they are least funny. And of course there's my film, *3 Ninjas* which every little kid laughed at because I told them they couldn't leave the movie house unless they did!

So that's it! Seven elements of theatre: Violence, Sex, Anticipation, Fear, Spectacle, Music, and Laughter all make up theatre. Drama is made up by everything that appeals to the mind: thoughts, words attitudes, morals and messages. Together, Drama and Theatre make up Entertainment. Now, I'm going to tell you a little story, a true story, that illustrates one important theatre and one drama. Here it is.

I once saw a preacher working to a small congregation made up mostly of small time sinners: prostitutes, drunks, dope addicts. I don't think there were any murderers or rapists in this crowd. The preacher put on a great act. He actually convinced the congregation that he was in direct contact with God and it they confessed their sins he could, with God's help, remove those ugly sins. So one by one he got the sinners to stand and confess (not me, I had no sins) and one by one he cleaned them. It took him about an hour to do that. It was amazing. He howled at the sinners and they cried. He blessed them and they cried. They cried together! After all of that he made an important announcement.

"Brother and sisters, tonight I have shown you the power of healing. I've taken your sins and thrown them to the four winds! Now, you've got to do your part! I can't do God's work without you. And your part is easy. What all of you have to is dig deep and be generous and the bread you cast upon the water will come back to you ten fold, nay it shall come back a hundred fold!"

And so to make a long story endless here, he passed around a collection plate. I saw these poor folks putting in quarters and dimes. I didn't put in anything. When the plate was passed back to Jones he began counting the collection in front of the congregation. When he finished it was clear that he wasn't pleased.

"How dare you insult me like this. How dare you insult God with a lousy $12.25. I can't do God's work on a stinkin' $12.25! You owe me more than a stupid $12.25! Now quit fooling around and come up with some serious bread!"

And with that he passed the plate around again. When he got it back the second time he counted it loudly right in front of everybody. And what do you think? Now, he had only twelve bucks. Somebody had lifted a quarter and replaced it with an army coat button. Well, I wanted to get a coke after the service! The pastor was furious! He screamed, he ranted, he jumped up and down like the wicked witch of the west!

"O.K. You want to play games, right?! O.K. We'll play! I showed you what my right could do now I'll show you what my left can do!"

He began grunting and puffing and suddenly he thrust his left hand down toward the floor! Suddenly a red light came on from someplace and it looked like his left hand was on fire. He began tugging on something . . . as if he were grabbing at a hand.

"Look at me, brothers and sisters! I'm grabbing the devil by my left hand. Look! I've got the devil by my left hand! And what do you think I'm going to do with my right hand? I'm going to reach into your bodies and pull out your souls and put them together with the devil."

And he called one of the drunks by name. The drunk stood up on wobbly legs. Jones screamed at him.

"What do you say, brother? You want me to put your soul in the hands of the devil? Do you?"

The drunk shook his head no. He was hypnotized.

"Then do God's work and fill up that plate!"

The drunk reached into his pocket and pulled out 3 dollars and threw it on the plate. Then Jones went back to everybody in the room with the same routine. I even gave back the quarter. When he counted the money again, he had $51.75. He put a big smile on his face.

"I knew you could do God's work! I knew you had it in you! I knew you would see the light! So, go and sin no more. Next week I'll be right here . . . and I know you'll be here too. We all got up and filed out. The group was quiet. Later, when I was in the car riding back home I began thinking, "Sometimes a crook can use God's name to steal."

So, did you get it? What is the theatre of the story? Well, there's no question but that the Pastor had a firm understanding of the theatrical element of fear! Yes, fear of the unknown. Fear of the devil! And of course the drama has got to be, "Sometimes a crook can use God's name to steal." That seems pretty obvious, right? And if you think about it there are other dramas that we could find here. You could say, "People are more afraid of the devil than of being poor." Sure, that works. The drama of the story comes out of the meaning of the ideas in the story and you're the one who can figure that out.

The next time you see some TV try to break it down into elements of theatre and drama. If you've got a kid watching *Sesame Street* notice the way that show tries to teach numbers. There is lots of spectacle and music. You see lots of color (spectacle), lots of sound effects and rhythm sounds (music). The drama of *Sesame Street* is "learn to count" and how we learn to count is the theatrical technique. The evening news does it the same way. Whether it be the local news or the national news it all begins with drama and continues on and one with theatre. Remember, drama always appeals to the brain and theatre always appeals to your emotions. Simple.

In Chapter Two we will examine how the Western World developed both Theatre and Drama. We will begin to investigate those dramatic elements and theatrical elements which have impact on us today. We will further add to our definitions of Theatre and Drama in our search for those things which entertain us or bore us. And we will discover something really important about entertainment; if you can feel the length of the drama or the theatre it is probably going to be boring! Right, time is the enemy of entertainment. Most of the time it is the drama of the entertainment that makes us feel that time is passing too slowly. All entertainment must make time stand still or it becomes very unentertaining!

CHAPTER ONE

Tear-out Study Guide

The following questions are important to your understanding of Chapter One. All of the answers can be found in Chapter One.

Fill in the blanks.

1. Entertainment is made up of _____ and _____.

2. Theatre appeals to the _____ and Drama appeals to the _____.

3. Violence is the number one element of _____.

4. Vicarious means to _____...

5. An idea is an example of _____.

6. Music appeals to our _____.

7. Time is the enemy of _____.

8. Anticipation asks the question, "_____?"

9. Seeking vengeance is part of _____.

10. There are _____ elements of Theatre.

It's Greek to
All of Us

In the Western world we attribute most of our appreciation for Drama and Theatre to the ancient Greeks. These great city states planted seeds for us 2,500 years ago which have flowered for centuries.

We think that Greek theatre came out of two experiences: the athletic experience and the religious experience. I say we *think* because nobody really knows how theatre started with the Greeks. But, there's a body of evidence which will allow us to make an educated guess. Some 600 years before the birth of Jesus the Greeks celebrated the existence of a half-god half-man named Dionyseus who apparently was a rather good natured fellow who reveled in wine, women and athletic competition. Most likely, an athletic contest, not far from Athens, took place every year. At the end of the contest a man or a replica of Dionyseus was carried to a place of celebration where songs and stories of glory were sung. Gradually these songs became more complex until people found as much interest in the ritual of celebrating Dionyseus' name as they did in celebrating the end of the games. Eventually the city fathers of Athens began paying choreographers to organize the poems and songs into a disciplined series of events which caught the imagination of the Greek men who attended these celebrations. Women were allowed to see the poetic songs but not perform in them because the ancient Greeks felt that women could not or should not be present at such important activities, not to mention that a lot of the performers were nude too!

Eventually the religious poems and songs became more sophisticated so by around 450 BC a Greek free man could go to a place that he called *"theatre"* (a place to see). It looked like a football stadium but with seating only for the home team. You looked down from the stands onto a playing surface where the actors played their parts. The average audience member sat with about twenty thousand others. At dawn drums would sound, horns would blow and out would glide sixty men dressed in headdresses, masks, and tall shoes. The actor stood about seven feet, far above the average height of the Greek. Within the mask there was a voice amplifier that the actor's voice was pushed through so that the voice seemed deep and resonant. All of these costume effects were designed to give the Greek a sense of visual spectacle . . . *theatre:* the spectacle of sixty men all moving with athletic grace, the size and power that the costumed image provided, and the shock of hearing the amplified voice. Yet for all of this Theatre the Greeks were far more interested in the Drama.

The first great Greek playwright was a man named Aeschylus. Aeschylus took the myths and legends of the gods and Greeks and gave them a sense of presence and meaning that they had never had before. For example, Aeschylus wrote a play called *Prometheus Bound* (sometimes simply called *Prometheus*) which was based on the ancient Greek legend on how the Greeks were given fire. Prometheus, a member of a race of creatures called Titans, took fire from Mt. Olympus and gave it to the Greeks which was in direct violation of Zeus' orders. When Zeus discovered what Prometheus had done he chained Prometheus to a rock and commanded a vulture to rip out the unfortunate Titan's liver every afternoon. The whole myth was acted and sung with such great power that we know the Greeks went crazy with delight after seeing the show.

In terms of our definitions of theatre and drama we can say that the myth itself is the drama. The moral message of the play is "don't mess with the gods ." That seems to be a standard message in many of the Greek plays; the Greeks knew that there was an order and control in the world and if you tamper with that control then you get punished. And there are dramatic messages here. For instance, Prometheus actually did a good deed by giving the Greeks fire even though he suffered for it. Therefore, another dramatic message could be, sometimes we are punished even for acts of kindness. Now, as we said before, the Greeks knew the myth and probably understood the dramatic message before they saw the play so what was the big thrill about seeing something which was not new to them? Remember, Theatre is *how* it is said. Of course, the message was old but the delivery of the message was very new and very exciting. The use of voice and movement riveted the audience's attention to the words of the play. The actors kept a constant change of masks at their disposal so the audience always had something new to observe and enjoy. To see Prometheus in a mask which represented his face as his liver was ripped out could have been quite exciting. And of course the liver of the actor was not ripped out but a red rag with a dark spot of brown was thrown around enough to convince the observers in the audience that the liver was indeed out of the body. Some of the men in the audience might have even reacted physically to such a terrible sight even though it was only symbolic of the actual thing. You see, the Greek used his imagination to see things that were suggested. The Greek could see the spectacle of the island where Prometheus was chained; the Greek could see the vulture flying overhead about to land on the poor captive. *Above all the Greek did not want to see actual violence on stage—he wanted to see pretend and symbolic violence.*

Now it seems that the Greek went to the theatre to see serious plays and that is not true. Before the serious play started he was treated to a *Satyr play*. It was much like watching a cartoon before the main attraction. The Satyr play was a sexual event which featured men wearing long phalluses (fake penises) chasing men pretending to be women disguising their genital parts. The whole idea is rather pornographic but remember, the Greeks did not want to see real sex on stage . . . only pretend sex. Now after the Satyr play was over, an actor or a playwright would enter the stage and declare in a loud voice that the play was going to begin and everybody ought to get a grip on himself. So, the form of comedy preceding tragedy much like a cartoon prepares the audience for a more thought provoking presentation.

The form of presentation began to change, however, with the rise of the playwright *Sophocles*. Sophocles reduced the size of the chorus, created more interesting stories, even though they were still based on historical events and myths. Sophocles was a greater playwright than Aeschylus because he wrote plays about honest to goodness heroes! While Aeschylus wrote plays about gods vs. gods, Sophocles wrote plays about gods and heroes. The Greeks could identify more with heroic types such as Oedipus, Herecles (Hercules), etc. He touched human qualities in his audience and developed them more dramatically. Let us take the most famous of his plays, *Oedipus Rex*. Sophocles draws upon the famous and tragic story of a baby named Oedipus who, according to the prophetic Delphi Oracle, was destined to marry his mother and murder his father. And what was worse he was supposed to have even fathered children by his own mother! The Greeks really thought the whole idea was a terrible curse and really disgusting and, therefore, good subject material for a play. As the play begins we learn that Oedipus' parents have tried to get rid of Oedipus by giving him to a family many miles away. However, after the baby grows up to manhood he discovers his terrible curse and runs away from home, thinking that if he stays he will end up doing something terrible! Naturally he runs away from home and goes right back to the city of Thebes, the original city of his birth, and meets his father. Of course he doesn't know it is his father and naturally he gets into a terrible fight with the old guy and kills him. The audience must have gone crazy yelling at Oedipus not to kill the old man but it doesn't do any good. By the time Oedipus gets around to killing the old man who is the King of Thebes the audience already knows that the drama of the piece is: you can't escape your fate. Well, Thebes needs a new King because the old one was mysteriously murdered. He can solve the riddle of the Sphinx, will become the new King and automatically marry the Queen, his mother. The audience is going crazy. Oedipus ends up fostering three children: two brother-sons and one sister-daughter. The Greeks hated incest and no doubt they were vomiting in their seats. But! The worst is yet to come! Oedipus thinks that it is his duty to find the murderer of the old King. Everybody tells him to forget it but he insists. So, after a ruthless investigation he finally has the name of the murderer. Horrified he learns that he is the murderer. And then he learns that his curse has come true. The truth, the recognition of his acts drives him crazy. In a fit of passion he rips out his eyes! The actor playing this part of Oedipus turned from the audience, took off his horror mask and slipped on a mask with trails of blood streaming from two black holes. The actor turned quickly to the audience and no doubt he heard screams from them when they saw this terrible mutilation.

The bizarre act of ripping one's eyes out created *Fear* in the audience, that wonderful theatrical element that seems to be universal in every person who has shuddered at the sight of somebody else's misfortune. The Greeks knew that Oedipus would end up trying to punish himself for something not in his control to change. The act of seeing Oedipus punish himself was so *violent* that the *Drama* was vividly brought to our eye through the use of the bloody mask. Do you think today that we would be shocked at the sight of a man's dismemberment? Possibly , if the dramatic values of the ideas and motivations were as shocking as the act itself. Certainly films like *Halloween* and *Friday The 13th* and on and on have made a great deal of money because they promise death and destruction.

Sophocles wrote many plays but there is only one more that I would like to discuss in this Chapter, *Philoctetes.* This play not only provides an intensely interesting story for us but it also expands our definition of *Theatre.* At this time add another term to our list from Chapter I: *Bravado.* Bravado means crazy pride bordering on insanity. Sophocles knew his Greeks very well. Being a small group of city states, they always seemed to be outnumbered by a foe, yet they always seemed to win their battles. How could they? What inside the Greek could have motivated this 4'9" hero who weighed about 100 lbs and had an average life span of 19 years to be so victorious? The Greeks of the 5th Century BC *knew* they could not be beaten! They psychologically knew that they were better than anybody else. The English went through that period in the 16th Century and we went through it during our 19th Century. Sophocles knew how well the Greeks loved supporting the underdog so in his play *Philoctetes,* he put forth the question: should a man be forced by the overwhelming odds of the state to do something that hurts his individuality even though he might be destroyed because he took an unpopular position. The story of Philoctetes must go down in history as one of the most interesting in the history of theatre.

It takes place during the Trojan War in which the Greeks, under the leadership of Memeleus and Agamemnon raised an army to attack Troy because the younger Prince of Troy, Paris, stole Memeleus' wife, Helen. Among the soldiers who traveled to Troy to help the Greeks seek vengeance was a man called Philoctetes. Philoctetes was distinguished by the bow and arrows that he carried since they were gifts of the demi-god, Herecles (Hercules). They were magic weapons. All Philoctetes had to do was call out the name of the victim and the bow and arrow would do the rest. With this formidable weapon Philoctetes was quite a favorite fellow among the Greeks.

Philoctetes was sailing across the Aegean Sea with Odysseus (Ulysses) when the boat needed to put into port at an island to take on water and food. Philoctetes decided to take a little walk about the island and stumbled onto a magic field of grass. The pasture belonged to the god Apollo. Philoctetes violated the spot with his presence, and Appolo sent a serpent to attack Philoctetes. The snake struck the poor man on the foot. A lump of poison began to travel up the leg and up the body toward the heart. At last the poison was about to reach the heart, and Philoctetes was in such pain that he was asking the gods for a swift death, *but* before the poison reached the heart it vanished. Picking himself off the ground, Philoctetes walked back to the ship just as it was about to set sail. On the ship Philoctetes was telling everybody how lucky he was to be alive when all of a sudden the curse started again and Philoctetes began to scream in pain. The Greeks aboard ship took this as a bad sign, a bad omen for the voyage, and they wanted to get rid of him. In order to save the expedition from a complete morale breakdown, Odysseus abandoned poor Philoctetes on a barren rock called Lemnos. For ten years Philoctetes struggled to stay alive on the rock island by shooting seagulls with his magic bow and arrows.

Ten years later an oracle proclaimed that the walls of Troy would not fall to the Greeks until the bow of Philoctetes would come to Troy in the hands of Philoctetes. The Greeks thought it over and sent Odysseus back to Lemnos with the son of the great hero Achilles, Neoptolemus. So, the Greeks sail back to the island where they find what is left of Philoctetes. The years have aged him. He is little better than an animal, suffering un-told agonies as every twenty minutes of his life he must experience the poison curse. When Neoptolemus sees the poor old thing, he tries to be gentle with him, but then Odysseus shows up and Philoctetes turns into a wild savage and tries to kill him, but he is now too weak even to seek vengeance. Odysseus tells Philoctetes that no matter what has happened to him, no matter what has been done to him, no matter how much he has suffered, that above all he is Greek and must follow orders. He tells Philoctetes that he must come back with him and go to Troy and do his duty. In one of those electric mo-ments that happens rarely in theatre, Philoctetes looks at Odysseus and says, "no ." Oh, the Greeks must have gone crazy when they heard Philoctetes say no to his General. Philoctetes, the man who had suffered so much against the greatest of odds, was now risk-ing the last little fragment of his dignity in a valiant attempt to withstand the ultimate au-thority, the state. Many of the Greeks in the audience muttered to themselves claiming that Sophocles had gone too far. "This is treason," someone might have shouted. Yet, in their hearts they respected Philoctetes for his bravery, for his *Bravado*. His bow was stolen from him during one of his mad fits and now he has been stripped of everything except his own Greek spirit. The conflict mounts, both on stage and in the audience. Then suddenly out of a mysterious hole beneath the stage, a strange image emerges. It is cov-ered with blood and earth and the audience members cannot believe their eyes. Sophocles wanted to shock his audience with an unexpected shade (ghost) from Hades. The visual shock was supposed to rivet the audience's attention on the action but what actually hap-pened was a riot. The audience trampled themselves trying to get out of the theatre. Several people died. Order was finally restored and the play continued. The visual shock, the spectacle of trying to scare the audience into paying attention, is still being used today. When the hero in *Raiders of the Lost Ark* is suddenly surprised by a huge boulder which is rolling down upon him, the audience watching the movie should begin to feel the vic-arious thrills of imminent danger. We think that the audience 450 years before the birth of Jesus, sitting in the ancient stone seats in the Greek theatre, experienced the same feelings as they watched Philoctetes looking up at the bloody figure rising up before him from the trap in the center of the theatre.

The ghost is Herecles, sent from Hades to solve the problem of the play. In true Greek fashion Herecles negotiates with both Odysseus and Philoctetes; in short, Philoctetes must go to Troy *but* the horrible curse is lifted. The play ends with everybody, especially the audience, happy.

Now, using our definitions of Theatre and Drama, we can see some very clearcut ideas emerging from *Philoctetes*. The Drama of the piece is very straightforward: *the state always wins*. The word or the moral or the attitude is completely wrapped up in the idea of duty. The Theatre becomes important when we see how Sophocles tries to make the idea of duty exciting and stimulating for the audience. When you go to a movie and you find it exciting because there are lots of visual effects but after a while the film becomes boring even though the effects are still going on, you can bet the drama of the film has broken down. If the story does not hold your interest because its dramatic value, meaning, is childish, then the theatre will only make the drama seem exciting for a short time. In other words, frosting is nice but, if that's all there is to eat, then there is a good chance you'll get sick to your stomach! Never underestimate the value of a good story.

Sophocles was a master story teller and a playwright who knew how to motivate the interest of his audience, but it is the playwright Euripides who actually combined the elements of drama and theatre for us so successfully that the movie producers are still copying his material and his theatrical techniques. What Euripides understood about human nature was man's need for lust, greed, avarice, human weakness, and lying: all the ingredients necessary for us to enjoy life. In the 5th Century B.C. play *Hypolitus,* Euripides develops a play out of the old story about the marriage of Thesus and Phaedra. It seems that Thesus, a big hero and King, decided to take a new wife. He chose a young little girl named Phaedra. Now Theses already had a son, Hypolitus, by a previous wife who was an Amazon. The boy grew up loving only hunting. He was shy and a bit awkward, but when he was in the jungle the kid was a tiger! When Thesus brought Phaedra into his house, he assumed they would all live together as one big happy family. Wrong. The moment Phaedra met Hypolitus two things happened: she fell in love with him and he fell in hate with her. Now, according to the Greeks incest covered any family relationship that resulted in intercourse, including step family members. Nevertheless, she wanted the boy and she tried to seduce him. He rejected her every time. One night, she sent for him and told him either he made love to her or she'd tell Thesus that he had tried to rape her. Hypolitus laughed at her and went out hunting by the ocean (I know there isn't much to hunt by an ocean, but that's the way the story goes). Phaedra rips up her clothes, and runs to Theses, tells him the lie that his son tried to rape his step-mother. Thesus doesn't even wait to verify the story; he immediately brings down a curse on his son. Out of the ocean a sea monster rises, scares Hypolitus' horse which throws the boy down on a rock and kills him. Meanwhile Thesus is starting to regret his curse when the news comes that Hypolitus is dead. He runs to tell Phaedra and finds her dead. She committed suicide because she had caused the curse. Thesus sits down and reflects on his bad luck. The audience reflects with him only they know something he doesn't know; none of this would have happened if he hadn't jumped to conclusions. The drama of the play emerges through recognition of the problem. In all ways this play combines the perfect elements of drama and theatre. First, we have a story which has tremendous dramatic value and a pot full of morals, attitudes, ideas, etc. *The plot, or sequence of events,* is easy to follow and just sexually permissive enough to hold your interest. All of the bloody and sensual descriptions are so theatrical that the ideas seem to be all painted in technicolor for you. The theatre is totally wrapped up in trying to excite your sense of outrage. From then on, playwrights have been trying to duplicate the same set of circumstances for an audience. Today, on TV, we have enough incest, fatherly foolishness, motherly shame, and basic lust, greed and avarice to keep the soap box opera watchers of America in heaven for years—decades!

Of course Euripides didn't know at the time that he was giving birth to such exciting and culturally enriching shows as *Dallas, Falcon's Crest,* and *The Young and the Restless* (had he dreamt of such a possibility he might have burnt his manuscripts) but we all have a debt to pay to him anyway. But even more than Euripides, Aristophanes did more to help us enjoy the overly serious moments in our lives. Mr. Aristophanes gave us satire, a theatrical element which helps us take our overly serious lives a little less seriously. Dramatically we can make a point and theatrically we can make that point interesting, right? Well, *satire* is a way of making a theatrical point by poking fun at something serious by taking one of the flaws of the serious thing and exaggerating it. For example, Aristophanes observed that Athens was embroiled in a terrible war with her Greek city-state neighbors. The war went on and on with no apparent end in sight. There seemed no way to negotiate a peace because none of the combatants was interested in making peace. Aristophanes satirized the war by creating the play, *Lysistrata.* Lysistrata was an Athenian woman who wanted to see the war stopped so she devised a play whereby all the women in Athens would deny their husbands sex until the men made peace. In other words nobody would get a piece until everybody got peace! Lysistrata enlisted the aid of the Spartan women in order to put the same pressure on the Spartan males. The Spartan males and the Athenian males took up the challenge and claimed that the women would give up before they would. By the end of the play the men are wrecks. They walk doubled over, they can't concentrate, and the last thing on their minds is making war; they would rather make anything but war!

Perhaps the most entertaining movie, TV play or stage play is a good satire. Take any serious subject, put it under a great deal of pressure until a weakness shows up and then exaggerate weakness and you've got *satire*. One of the best ones on the market today is *Hardware Wars*! *Hardware Wars* takes all of the visual impact of *Star Wars* and reduces it to simple laughter—an excellent film and a very funny one. *Remember* when you are laughing time passes quickly, so quickly you're not even aware that the jokes are three thousand years old and the satirical style was created to attack the most universal problem we have in the world today—war.

CHAPTER TWO

Tear-out Study Guide

Fill in the blanks.

1. The Greeks loved _____ violence.

2. Theatre means _____ according to the Greeks.

3. The first Greek playwright was named _____.

4. He wrote a play called _____.

5. A Satyr Play is a _____.

6. Sophocles wrote a play called _____ which resulted in the central character ripping out his eyes.

7. "You can't escape your fate" is an example of _____, not theatre.

8. "The state always wins" is a drama of _____.

9. A sequence of events is called a _____.

10. Hypolitus was written by _____.

Roman Theatre, Death Do Us Part

Romans laughed too. They laughed as they conquered the Greeks. But the Greeks got even, they introduced the Romans to theatre and in the end the Romans were destroyed by it. Ok, I can hear you now, "theatre can't conquer anybody! Theatre can't destroy anybody!" Well, in this case you're wrong, that's exactly what happened and what is worse we, you and I, inherited all the wrong, the brutal, the love of cruelty that was characteristic of Roman theatre. First of all, you can't realize how much impact Roman culture had on us. The Roman empire which lasted from about 250 BC to 476 AD made its impact on us in the most important way one culture can affect—through the pocket book. Nearly everything we have learned about capitalism was first begun by the Romans including making a profit on theatre. We think that the first Roman theatre was merely an imitation of the Greeks but I disagree with that theory. I believe the first Roman theatre took place at high noon in the city of Rome during the busiest market day of the year. Two hundred fifty years before the execution of Jesus, Romans were selling and buying like crazy. The pressure of competition was so great that I feel it was certain that some enterprising Roman salesperson tried to sell his products with aid of some theatrical device. Perhaps he set up a stand and tried to sell a magic cure-all (no doubt Rubican water, straight from Northern Italy, good for what ails ya) by singing a jingle, such as:

> "Rubican water is the best of all,
> Makes tall men short and short men tall."

It probably sounds a lot better in Latin. Anyway, the theatrical device of singing no doubt drew a crowd and soon the crowd began looking forward more to the "commercial" approach to theatre than they did to buying the product. But do you see what we're pointing to here? The Romans did understand the value of slicking up a package so that it would sell faster. Turn on your TVs and see what happens every eight and a half minutes: *Roman Theatre.* Info-commercials might have been created by the Romans!

Although the Greeks made an excellent ritual and a wonderful competition out of their theatre, the Romans ignored those noble endeavors and turned professional theatre into a profitable business. First, we need to discuss Roman comedy since the characters that they invented are still around today making money for everybody. The silly little comedies that the Romans invented were all patterned after the comedies of the Roman Therrence (who stole them from the Greek Plautus; Romans were very original with everybody else's work) who created such interesting characters as the Braggart Warrior, the silly but wise-cracking Servant, the Leacherous Old Man, the Sexy Young Lady, the Sexy Young Man, and the Too Smart Housewife. Wait a minute, you say you never heard of these characters? You say you never want to hear of these characters? Too late, they're still here. Two thousand years later and Roman Comedy is still making money. For example, the Braggart Warrior was a pig-headed opinionated individual—bigoted, self-righteous, not very bright but thinks he knows everything—who is it? Give up? Homer on the *Simpsons*. Right out of the Roman mold! What with re-runs nearly everybody in the country who watches TV is treated to a two thousand year old performance everyday (twice a day if you own cable). And of course we scream with laughter at the servant who puts down the master or at least we all seemed to enjoy *Nanny*, or if you are old enough to remember or young enough to order cable then you recognize Peter on *Bachelor Father* as the Chinese example of the Roman creation of the American comic servant. The leacherous Old Man is none other than Louis on *Taxi*. The Sexy Young Woman can be none other than Lonnie Anderson on *WKRP*, or dozens of others on prime-bust TV. The Sexy Young Man could be the Fonz, and the too smart Housewife is perhaps the most durable and beloved character of TV screen, Lucy. And Roseanne on the *Roseanne* show is a combination of the Braggart Warrior and the wise-ass servant.

If you think it was all fun and games in the Roman Theatre then think again. In your history classes and in some of your Drama classes your teachers all talk about the greatness of Roman Drama which included the great poets Seneca, Terrence, Virgil, etc. However, more important than *Drama* was the *Theatre*. Something sick, degenerate, and very inhuman developed in Roman Theatre and along with the harmless comedy sit-com characters this disease was also passed along to us. This disgusting and completely degenerate theatrical attitude developed as a direct result of permissive violence. It was the Coliseum, the grand arena that housed a hundred thousand people, that allowed the Roman imagination to give vent to any and every atrocity. During the First Century AD the Romans found the ultimate theatrical event: Death. It first began as athletic competition; one man would pit his skill and strength against another in combat. The Roman audience would pay to see this just as we pay to see football or boxing. At first the end result of the athletic event was to disarm one of the athletes, but soon the crowds demanded more excitement from the entertainment. The thrill of combat was only as thrilling as the event was unpredictable. As soon as there was a chance that the crowd could predict the end result of the competition, then the crowd lost interest and demanded more challenging theatre . . . the administration cooperated.

By the middle of the First Century such Roman Emperors as Caligula and Nero (rather exotic homicidal idiots) provided such entertainment as men being dragged from horses (very popular among the rural crowds), lions eating Christians, Jews and assorted weak minorities. At last the Romans found the ultimate sport: real warfare. The Coliseum could be flooded and then accommodate Roman warships loaded with soldiers who would then make war with each other . . . to the death. Death is the key word here. Within our natures there is something fascinating and theatrical about the act of death. We watch things die out of curiosity, out of cruelty, out of boredom. We go to the movies and become transfixed as we watch a tiger stalk a young deer. We know that the end result will be a sudden rush at the prey, a scuffle and a possible attack. We watch with horror as the tiger dashes through the jungles on the outskirts of Bombay charging the unsuspecting prey. Or even better yet, the poor prey realizes that it is about to be eaten and hopelessly bolts for freedom. We are thrilled and horrified when at last the carnivore corners and crushes its prey. We are no different than that Roman citizen watching with horror and glee as the lion corners the Christian and then leaps for the throat of its victim. A roar goes up from the crowd as blood and bone splatter and bounce about the arena. Theatre.

Today, there are dozens of Roman movies highlighting the best in gore, murder, frenzy and maximum violence. *Visiting Hours* features a sick little boy who grows up into a sick big man who uses a knife to scare the life out of you in the audience. *Halloween* and *Halloween II* show enough blood and bone to get you through medical school. The list goes on and on because we inherited from our Roman ancestors the need to see this kind of entertainment. Even in the Roman Classical theatre we have more violence and terror than the Greeks would have ever tolerated. Seneca was a first Century playwright who wrote a play called *Thyestes*. It basically takes its story from the Greek myth about the curse of the house of Atreus. The upshot of the play is this: a brother invites his brother to dinner and then serves the brother his own children as haute entree. Disgusting? Terrible? Barbaric? Yes. Of course it is and don't forget *Theatrical* too.

Now this is not to say that the Romans *only* enjoyed terrible violence. That is wrong. They enjoyed classical Greek theatre, Roman contemporary melodrama (similar to our Soap Operas): light comedy, filthy comedy, political satire and modern tragedy. *But*, the heavyweight moneymaker, the sensational box office smash was always *theatre of death*. *On Golden Pond* was a beautiful movie about an old man who reestablishes a love relationship with his daughter that received much critical acclaim but it was *Paradise,* an inexpensive little horror film which, most critics agreed, had little or no social redeeming qualities which made infinitely more money because the gore content in that film reached even Roman expectations. Now you must ask a crucial question at this time. Why does filth and gore attract the general population more than honest and artistic endeavor? Why does violence seem more interesting to us than the passive presentation of magnificent poetry?

I think I have the answer. It has to do with evolution. Intellectually, many of us have evolved, but emotionally, few of us have advanced past the Roman period. *Natural Born Killers* is a great example of what film directors think you want to see!

They think that emotionally we are still looking for the same thrills that our two thousand year old ancestors looked for. After all, two thousand years is not much considering the age of man on this planet. From the moment the Roman yelled for delight at the prospect of a man dying in the arena to the present day is simply a wink of an eye. We are, in every emotional way what we were two thousand years ago. Ancient history is not so ancient after all, and theatre is still theatre regardless of two thousand years of sophistication. Change can only come when we reject violence.

At this point I would like to digress for a few moments and discuss an issue which really has little to do directly with theatre and drama. It has to do with the concept that America is the new Rome. Of course we can prove that our theatrical values concerning popular theatre are nearly the same but the question is are we really carbon copies of our Roman ancestors? Many historians think this is true. As the Romans destroyed themselves because they couldn't control the permissiveness of their society, so too are we on the same path to destruction. Pornography two thousand years ago was essentially the same kind of pornography that motivated the production of *Deep Throat* several years ago followed by countless other highly popular and commercially successful pornographic movies. But does this mean that our societies are twin cultures both heading to the brink of disaster in the same way? Well, I am here to say *No!* And I can prove it. We are not going the same way as the ancient Romans because our society has developed an entirely different set of values. For example, in the last days of the Romans, about 476 AD, the ancient Romans were so heavily invested in drugs that children were destroying themselves with narcotics and it is a fact that in our society drugs are . . . wait a minute. That was just a bad example. We are not going the same way as the ancient Romans because the Roman political system eventually became so corrupt that one could never trust an elected official to act legally and responsibly, and we all know that in our society politicians always act with honesty and . . . wait a minute. That's just a bad example. Here, this is better. In ancient Rome, near the end of the empire, the middle-class individual was practically destroyed, his money was eroded because of a high inflation rate, and it was nearly impossible for him to even buy a house, and we know that in our society that anybody can buiy a house and . . . well, that's just another bad example . . . this is it . . . this is it, in Rome when things were at their worst people would not trust each other. They had no respect for each other. In fact, if you suddenly turned out all the lights in ancient Rome, they would have looted each other like crazy and we all know that in our society that couldn't possibly happen. I mean if suddenly all the lights in New York City shorted out and the city was plunged in darkness there would be absolutely no looting and . . . Oh. Just another bad example, that's all. This is it. This will prove once and for all that in no way do we resemble the ancient

Romans and their problems. At the end of the Roman Empire the family unit was completely disregarded. Divorce was a way of life and we all know that in our society once people marry they never dream of div . . . Hm. Well, at any rate I think I have shown you why in no way do we resemble the ancient Romans and, therefore, most certainly we will not be destroyed in the same way. Count on it.

Wait a minute, I can hear you saying, "Regardless of all that philosophy stuff the fact remains Professor EmanuEl that people don't go to an arena and watch people die! Movies aren't real." My answer to you is this. For less than fifty dollars ($49.95) you can write to an address and the company that does business at that address will send you a "snuff" film. And what is the infamous "snuff film"? Very simply the actual deaths of people captured on video for your viewing disgust. Yes, for just a few dollars you can sit in the privacy of your own home, or in the darkness of your own personal closet and watch people die. You can see people who are being executed in Viet Nam, electrocuted in State prisons, hanged in Iran, shot to death by police from various countries and suicide victims from all over the world. Real people dying right before your eyes over and over again! Very Roman. Very American. Obviously somebody is keeping this company going since they've been in business since 1975. And if that's not enough just read your newspaper and watch your TV. Death is all around us and it finds its way to us via the most interesting mass media communication networks that we have. Every time a newscaster begins the story by saying, "The pictures you are about to see may not be suitable for young people because of their violent and graphic nature . . ." then you know the media is making entertainment money out of violence. Otherwise, they wouldn't show these pictures. But they know that *you* want to see them. Don't you remember how the TV stations played the beating of certain suspected criminal by the LA police over and over until you were sick to death of seeing it? And of course the pictures *form* the most famous murder case in the last fifty years are played over and over again because the media thinks that you are excited by them. Are they wrong? Are you excited? The honest answer to the last question tells us exactly how we feel about Roman violence. Violence held up to the public view for profit!

CHAPTER THREE

Tear-out Study Guide

1. The Romans like to see _____ violence on stage.

2. Seneca wrote a play called _____.

3. The Roman Empire lasted from _____ to _____.

4. The Romans made a big business doing theatre by building a _____.

5. A Roman Character who is pigheaded and opinionated is called _____.

6. Where can you see Roman Comedy today? _____

7. The ultimate entertainment goal of Roman coliseum theatre was for the audience to watch people _____.

8. Terrence was a Roman playwright who wrote _____.

9. Roman coliseum theatre first began as _____ pitting one man against another.

10. We can see an example of Roman violence in the movie _____.

Theatre and Drama
in the Dark Ages

After the fall of the Roman Empire, about 476 AD the Western world was plunged into a dark age. I always think of this as a giant hand from someplace beyond our galaxy snapping off the sun and figuratively that isn't too far off. Suddenly, without the Roman peace keeping force, the Western world was thrown into chaos. Law and order on a world wide scale ceased to exist. Each man was responsible for his own well-being since he couldn't count on a temporal authority to help him. The Catholic Church, however, guaranteed every son and daughter a place in the eternal hereafter. With the pain and suffering that characterized the average man's life, looking forward to a pleasant life after death was man's only ambition. Science and the arts had no place in this wild and jungle-like world society. Theatre was branded as the "devil's tool." Actors and playwrights were banned from society. The Catholic Church feared that the licentiousness of Roman theatre would undermine the religious doctrines of the Church, and with its customary attitude toward anything that might be considered anti-Catholic the Church damned theatre with the threat of excommunication for its players in the next world and bonfires for them in the present world. With the exception of jugglers, singers, a few dancers and a magician or two, the theatre business was through. But it is impossible to crush entertainment. It is impossible to force people not to want to be entertained. Maybe even more than the Roman Circus, people during the Dark Ages learned to enjoy the theatrical events of singing, jousting, and athletics. For six hundred years theatre stood still, and then, ironically, the Church itself helped bring theatre back to the world.

The only source of theatrical presentation in Europe was the Church Mass. The poor and the hungry as well as the somewhat affluent would gather in the dark structure that represented holy salvation and witness the Latin Mass. One day during the tenth Century in a small church right before Corpus Christi Day, one of the priests conducting the service must have stopped and thought for a moment and then uttered the words that gave theatre and drama a brand new life, a rebirth, a renaissance: "Quem Queretas." The congregation must have been dumb struck when they heard the strange digression from the litany that they had heard for years and years. "Quem Queretas," or "Where is He"? . . . the priest repeated. The congregation or audience sat silent and in awe to hear the priest who for years had been content to speak only the words that had been repeated for centuries. "Where is He"? He has risen is the answer. He is in heaven is the answer. He waits for us is the answer. He died for our sins is the answer.

Now the above is of course only speculation. We do know that sometime in the 10th century the Corpus Christi Mass was introduced to Europe and we do know that the Church approved of it and we do know that every year the Corpus Christi Mass became more complex and more complex. At last by the 13th Century the Corpus Christi Mass might have looked and sounded something like this:

It is late April and we are in a little country church outside of Paris. It is hot, muggy, maybe raining too. From all over the countryside hundreds have flocked to this little church that holds maybe three hundred men and women. For maybe an hour they have been sitting in the stuffy church. Crowded, wet, hot the congregation anticipates an exciting event. Slowly the church doors close and the creaking around of the rusty hinges ushers two priests to the holy Eucharist Table. They are dressed in the garb of High Mass. They are dimly lit since only candles are used to illuminate the scene. Preliminary prayers are made and then, about fifteen minutes later a drum is heard outside the church coupled with the sound of chains being dragged on stone. Suddenly, the doors of the church swing open and there standing in the doorway is the silhouette of a man, stripped naked except for a loincloth. The congregation tries to view him clearly but because of the rear lighting of the subject he seems to be nothing but a black outline. Slowly the naked person steps into the interior of the church and for the first time the congregation gets a clear look at him. He is a sorry sight. His body has been beaten; there are bloody bruises on his side. His body is bent because of one huge hewn cross he is carrying on his back. His feet are naked and leave bloody tracks when he walks. On his head a crown of thorns has been forced down and the trickles of blood find their way down his face, to his chin and then drop rhythmically to the stone floor of the church. Outside the church a chant is heard. Every step the bloodied man takes is matched with a drum beat, one chime of a bell. The congregation is transfixed. Some begin to cry. Others reach out and try to touch him. Slowly the figure reaches the front of the church and turns around. At the same time two non-descript figures remove the burden of the cross and the figure stands there before the people with his eyes raised toward heaven. One of the priests steps up to the congregation and asks the congregation if they would have this man spared from crucifixion. There is no answer. The other priest moves his hands in a circular fashion and proclaims, "his blood is upon your heads, I wash my hands of it" The other priest signals the non-descript figures and they raise the cross up behind the figure again. The first priest asks the question again, "Shall he be saved or shall the thief be saved?" No answer. "I take your silence condemns the man (he points to the man standing before the cross)." The non-descript figures lift iron nails above the figure standing before the cross and he extended both hands and assumed the position of crucifixion. They mime the nails being struck and the figure on the cross screams out in pain. First the left hand feels the nail and then the right. One of the non-descript takes the feet and mimes a nail going through them and another scream fills the church. Then, finally, one of the non-descript mimes a spear piercing the right side of the body and the Jesus figure on the cross suffering the agony of sacrifice and they are experiencing a dramatic presentation which not only touches their eyes and ears but their very souls. At last the figure on the cross begins to reach the end of his endurance. He lifts his eyes to the ceiling of the church and screams, "My God, My God, why have You forsaken Me" and then "Forgive them, they know not what they do" and then at last, "It is finished" and with the last line there comes such a scream that it nearly cracks the walls of the church.

It is a familiar scream to us. It is the same scream that came from the lips of the Greek actor playing Oedipus, it is the same scream that passed between the lips of the dying Roman soldier in the Arena, it is the same theatrical scream that had sounded for fifteen hundred years, and has now found its way within the sacred walls of the Holy Roman Church. How ironic that the Church that killed off theatre for six hundred years was responsible for bringing it back to the Western World. And it came back in a big way. The churches and the markets in front of the churches became the theaters for theatre and drama in the Dark Ages. They were known as Passion Plays, Mystery Plays, and the Miracle Plays. These plays glorified the Catholic Church and Bible and put the *fear* of damnation in the hearts of the viewers!

Now let us see what we have learned there and try to make it practical for us. First it is clear that we enjoy a good story with a moral to it. Take one of the most popular motion pictures of all time, *E.T.*. What really makes that film wonderful is the sense that love can win out over all. Right? The motion picture actually makes you love a plastic machine that has no human parts. Yet we, in our human way, overlay the heart and soul on the E.T. so it is possible for us to forget that it is simply a machine and love it. We cry a bit as we think the E.T. is dying and we cheer when we feel that the E.T. is about to go home and we cry again when the E.T. has to leave his little friend behind. Why do we enjoy these changes of emotions which are based on moral decisions? Because the Greeks taught us to appreciate such values. From Aeschylus to Sophocles to Euripides we learn that moral feelings keep our interest. Somewhere in our human nature there is a need to feel love, pain, sympathy and then watch it portrayed by somebody else so that we experience *vicarious* love, hate, sympathy and in the case of *E.T.* "ouch!" Then we have the Roman theatrical experience which releases the base instincts of violence and death. Do not deny these feelings. We are violent creatures and the Romans created an entire theatrical event out of the death of an individual. What we inherited from the Romans was *curiosity*. All a movie distributor has to do is suggest that there is a new high in blood, a new low in kindness, a new high in violence, a new low in charity, and we will flock to see the film whether it is good or bad by dramatic terms. Most of the time the Roman experience without the Greek experience is not satisfying. In other words, theatre without drama doesn't make us totally happy. Why? Because there is a touch of the better in all of us and when movies or plays try to bring that out by making us appreciate life and its complexities we are supremely entertained. So how now does theatre and drama in the Dark Ages fit into

all of this? *Fear* of the unknown is a very powerful theatrical tool. Fear of God's anger
. . . or the devil's anger is scary The theaters of the Dark Ages featured Hell Mouths . . .
or large representations of the entrance to hell! The Dark Age audiences saw smoke and
demons dancing around the Hell Mouth. It scared them! And it entertained them. The
Dark Ages actually combined in some ways Greek Drama and Roman Theatre!

How did we get out of those Dark Ages? Well, historians say that when the Spanish
houses of Castile and Aragon married and began to kick the Moors out of Spain in *1469*
. . . Forget it! We began to lose the Dark Ages when we rediscovered the ancient Greek
and Roman cultures! And of much of that discovery was through the re-discovery of the
Greek plays and Roman architecture! The Renaissance (the re-birth) of Europe came
through identifying with the Greeks and Romans whose civilizations had lay hidden for
fourteen hundred years! Or in short, the education lamp was lit when we began to take
pride in the glory and the excitement of the past!

CHAPTER FOUR

Tear-out Study Guide

1. The _____ destroyed Theatre and Drama.

2. The _____ brought back Theatre and Drama.

3. The Corpus Christi Day Mass eventually became _____.

4. Some of the plays of the Dark Ages were called _____.

5. The element as Theatre called _____ comes out of this period.

6. According to most historians the Dark Ages came to an end in the year _____.

7. The Roman Empire fell in about the year _____.

8. The power of the Roman Empire was replaced by _____.

9. A Hell Mouth was _____.

10. According to this chapter we came out of the Dark Ages when we began

    _____.

Shakespeare!

Wait a minute! I know exactly what you're going to say; you hate Shakespeare, your English teacher made you read Hamlet, and you didn't understand a word! Right? And what made it worse is that the English teacher kept telling you how wonderful it all was and how you would be all better people for the reading of it, right? And this really probably made you miserable; somewhere during the year the teacher dragged you to a Shakespeare production and all you saw were a bunch of strange little fellows jumping around in tights waving fake swords and you were so bored and angry because you could have been home that night watching *Martin*. O.K., I understand. You had a bad experience but just remember that the experience was bad, Shakespeare wasn't! You can take the most exciting plays in the world and make them dull if you forget the elements of drama and theatre. And let me tell you right now there is more Shakespeare in us and in our values about life than we get from any other playwright in the history of the world. What we learned from Shakespeare made *Raiders of the Lost Ark* possible as well as *Poltergeist* and any number of films and plays which have captured our imagination because of their bravery and innovation. Read on and we will open your eyes and perhaps turn you on to a whole new and exciting playgoing experience.

First we must understand that I'm going to ignore an entire form of theatre called Italian Renaissance which included Comedia Del Arte, a wonderful form of theatre based on Roman Comedy. I do this because I think the Elizabethan Shakespeare period had more influences on us. If you are at all interested in Roman Comedy, however, you ought to really study this period from 1485–1600, it will really excite you. So, let us now turn to what I think is the most important period in the history of entertainment, Shakespeare and the Elizabethans.

In 1558 Elizabeth Tudor, a somewhat illegitimate daughter of King Henry VIII, became queen. She was an incredible woman, perhaps the greatest monarch Britain ever had. She was tough, honest, brilliant and very English. She was first, last, and always an English person and she motivated a feeling of English chauvinism called the Elizabethan Period. It was a time when the English were coming out of their dark ages into a magnificent renaissance, a rebirth of thinking, science, exploration, and art.

And it all hinged on belief in the ultimate destiny of the anglo to rule the world! Manifest destiny. In some ways America inherited that need to be the best, the most powerful, the most successful. After all, most of the founding fathers of the USA were trained in this sense of anglo destiny. But what is really important here is the sense that the Elizabethan (Elizabethan was so popular that she gave her name to the period that marks her rule) assumed that he would be victorious . . . no matter what the odds! This attitude was positive for the Elizabethans but negative for everybody else because there is an inherent attitude of racism in this manifest destiny. The Elizabethans thought they were better than any other culture on earth. They thought they were better because of who they were and who the rest of the people on earth were . . . no other reason. This is racism. Superiority based on race. Not many people took this superhuman attitude that the Elizabethans cherished for themselves until the year 1588 when a very tiny English navy soundly defeated a huge Spanish armada made up of nearly 500 ships. Suddenly the world viewed the Elizabethans with a new respect . . . and fear. Since Britain was such a tiny nation they always fought against overwhelming odds . . . and most of the time they won. Great legends grew up around this sense of power. There's even a word that describes this behavior: *Bravado.* Bravado means, crazy courage bordering on insanity.

Let's examine Queen Elizabeth I's actions when she was courted by King Phillip of Spain. He begged her to marry him. He didn't really want to marry her as much as he wanted to control England and increase his power in the world. Elizabeth could have married him and increased her power in the world as his wife . . . or take a big chance and refuse to marry him and try to advance England's power by risking war with Spain and defeating the Spanish. If Vegas were giving odds on a war between powerful Spain and upstart England you could get a fifty point spread! And probably most people would bet on Spain to defeat England by 51 points! Well, you all ready know that Elizabeth refused to marry Phillip and the two nations went to war. One of the great bravado stories of the time was this. Admiral Sir Francis Drake was lawn bowling on the banks of the Thames river when he heard the news that a mighty armada of nearly five hundred ships was about to invade England . . . they were only a short distance away. Drake, according to the legend, stopped the messenger from giving him anymore details until he finished his game. When he heard that he was only outnumbered ten to one he started a new game! Bravado! Well, you know what happened. England destroyed the Spanish navy and suddenly became a terrifyingly powerful nation . . . terrifying to the rest of the world because England served notice on the other nations; here we come . . . ready or not. The Elizabethans were very tough. Tougher than any of us could imagine. One of their favorite sports was called bull-baiting. A full grown bull was set loose in a bull ring. Bulldogs ripped and tore at the bull's legs and stomach until the bull killed them. Then, any Elizabethan could jump into the ring and kill the bull . . . and of course, risk being killed! The risk is what made the game exciting! Now, out of that violence loving, racist, action based, vibrant society came William Shakespeare.

Shakespeare, a product of the village of Stratford on Avon, came to London in the 1580's ready to advance his career as a writer or an actor or a . . . well, in London you could do anything you wanted and be anything you wanted except a loser. Bravado demanded that no matter what Shakespeare did he would have to be a winner. My God, what an exciting day it was for Shakespeare the day he arrived London. If he crossed London Bridge he would be treated to the sight of decapitated heads stuck on pikes . . . traitors to Queen Elizabeth. The city would have been a beehive of activity. The ale flowed like water over a dam, the theaters were packed. The bull-baiting rings were equally packed. The whorehouses were doing a, you should excuse the expression, bang-up business. Fights broke out on every corner. Honor was defended with fists and swords. Shakespeare must have loved the carnival-like streets of London; looking out for the garbage thrown out the second story windows; wandering minstrels singing and playing for coins, buskers of all kinds trying to make a living by their talents, jugglers, street musicians, story tellers, and fire eaters. Acrobats, dancers, tightrope walkers, and knife throwers. Shakespeare must have rubbed shoulders with the mighty and the powerful. He watched the whole of English society buzzing back and forth across the Thames. What a shock it must have been for a country boy suddenly to see what city life was all about. It must have thrilled him and maybe scared him as well. But what was most important for a potentially great playwright, perhaps the greatest playwright of the western world, here was a population that was made up of the *best of Greek and Roman values.* The Elizabethans had that love of literature and story telling that was so inherently Greek and that love of exciting violence that the Romans loved if an actor on stage was killed in a sword fight (we mean that his character was killed) the Elizabethan actor would open his leather vest and show his guts falling out. In the Roman period it probably would have been his own but in the Elizabethan period it was sheep guts! The effect was terrifying . . . but not harmful to the actor! And of course Elizabethans loved plays which clearly defined right and wrong . . . and the right always triumphed over evil! Bad people were punished and good people were rewarded. Morality was clearly defined. But it was defined by men . . . no women were allowed to act!

So now we get down to the question; why were the Elizabethans so crazy for their theatre? There were many reasons and all of them have contributed to our enjoyment of theatre today. First of all, smart Mr. Shakespeare understood what entertained his audience and what still entertains you and me. The first thing he tried to do in most of his plays was scare his audience. He knew that the thrill of being made afraid is a response that we human beings are born with and never lose. He frightened most of his audiences with the "unknown." Ghosts and witches turned his audiences to jelly. They really believed in ghosts. They had scientific evidence that ghosts existed. And ghosts were definitely hazardous to your health. Nevertheless, the audiences always loved being exposed to them just for the thrill of it all. Alright, I can hear you now saying, "I don't believe in ghosts and they don't scare me." Right. How many of you saw *Poltergeist* and were jumping out of your seats every time a ghost (which you don't believe in) hit the screen? The Elizabethan audience thought that a ghost could rise out of the ground at any time, grab a person and then drag him straight to hell. Scary. Of course they didn't run around wondering when the next dragging was going to take place. If you're having trouble understanding this then maybe this will make sense to you. In our everyday lives we live with the threat of cancer. It can hit us from smoke, drink, or food. And it is a real threat and a real danger to us (just as ghosts were a real threat to the Elizabethans) yet we don't run around changing our lives because we know that cancer is an ever present danger.

The other item of fear that Shakespeare used was the witch. Elizabethans were positive that witches were walking among them, most of them disguised as old women, but not all. The Devil, thought the Elizabethan, could turn the most beautiful woman and the most handsome man into a witch. And if you say, "yeah, but I'm not afraid of witches", then all you have to do is think about how you feel about aliens from foreign planets. All of you rush to the theatre to see *The Thing* or *E.T.* in hopes that your imaginations will allow you to believe that strange visitors from another planet are really here among us.

Besides those two devices Shakespeare really knew how to do other things that we appreciate today. First, he could really tell a super story. All of his plays deal with adventure in some form or another. *Raiders of the Lost Ark* contains Shakespearean elements: supernatural elements, heroic people, evil villains and plenty of violence all wrapped up in a tight plot. If you really see a great production of *Macbeth* then you know that Shakespeare was a 16th–17th Century Steven Spielberg (or vice-versa might be more appropriate). The ability to tell a great story and to make the audience use their imagination while watching the play made Shakespeare the best playwright of their period and our period.

I think that rather than just carry on about how great Shakespeare is we ought to examine one of his plays the way it ought to be produced so that you can see exactly what I'm talking about. Notice, I didn't say we ought to *read* one of his plays. Shakespeare did not write his plays to be read and studied as pieces of literature, as pieces of *Drama*. He didn't actually even want his plays read by anybody. He was a director and producer of plays which he wanted to make money. O.K., is that clear? We're talking entertainment here, not education. It is wonderful that education is a product of this kind of entertainment, but it wasn't Shakespeare's prime reason for writing and producing. So, let us now take two of his plays which offer us a great deal, and discuss them and see if there is anything for us to learn about our own tastes in theatre and drama. The first under discussion is *Macbeth*. Come on, resist the temptation to jump the next few pages and play along with me for a few minutes.

Macbeth was basically written to give his audience a giant "boo" and scare them out of ten years' growth. It was produced in the early part of the 17th Century (around 1606) and featured a character in it named Banquo, a Scottish noble to whom James the First, the monarch who followed Elizabeth, was related. Shakespeare thought he could continue to get royal patronage if he wrote about a subject near and dear to the history of the new King. At any rate the play begins sometime long ago, long before there were any

Elizabethans, long before there was even an England united under one secure monarch. It takes place in a wild and foreign land somewhere in Scotland. At the beginning of the play Scotland is being torn both by civil war and invasions from the Vikings. One figure stands above all in his ferocious protection of homeland; Macbeth. The King of Scotland, Duncan, learns that Macbeth has slaughtered hundreds of the invaders and has also nearly singlehandedly, with the exception of help from his close friend Banquo, put down the civil war. Duncan is pleased and he sends a messenger out to find Macbeth so that Macbeth and Banquo can be rewarded for their heroism. Meanwhile, in a dangerous swamp somewhere near the battlefield where Macbeth has shown his fidelity to king and country, the earth cracks open and amidst thunder and lightning three messengers from hell slip and ooze their way to the surface of the earth and crawl along the stage floor toward the audience. My God, there must have been some kind of panic when all of a sudden these three messengers from the devil magically take on human form and begin to speak or chant. And why are they here, why have they come to the world of man to seek somebody? They want to test somebody. They no doubt found their way into the audience, causing a near riot as they constantly reach out and examine the people trying to avoid their touch at all costs. And then it becomes clear that the one person these slimy spirits are looking for is Macbeth. They've come to challenge the best. They are going to offer him power, immortality and complete dominance over those around him, if he will only change his character and become evil. At first, when Macbeth sees the evil shades, he mistakes them for just strange old women. But the boiling pot of snake eyes and lizard tails convinces him that they may be more than just members of the local senior citizens club out for a picnic. Then the leader of this band of creepy crawlers claims that Macbeth will first be promoted to a high position in the kingdom, and then he will be king, and then then they point at Banquo and claim that his children will be kings (James the First must have loved that part). The witches vanish but we can still hear their haunting laughter as Macbeth *is* promoted just the way the witches said. And now Macbeth begins to wonder, could the witches be right? Just as they predicted, he has risen in power, but how could he become king? First there is the old king and second he has two sons. He writes everything that has happened in a letter and sends it off to his wife, Lady Macbeth, but believe me she is no "lady." When she reads the letter, everything becomes clear. The witches have predicted ultimate power for her husband which also means ultimate power to her. Macbeth, however, is too good to see the easiest way to secure that power . . . eliminate the king and his two sons. In one of the scariest scenes in the play she calls upon the forces of darkness to "unsex" her there and turn her into something that she is not so that she will have the strength and power to destroy Duncan and his sons. And as soon as she calls down evil to help her, evil responds. When you ask for trouble there is always somebody or something to help you out. And faster than you can say "Exorcist" she is possessed. As soon as Macbeth comes home he notices that his wife has changed quite a bit.

And when he hears that she has a plan for both of them becoming king and queen he is sure that she has changed. And when he finds out that the king is coming to stay at his castle and reward him for his brave acts during the recent war, he begins to understand that his wife wants him to commit murder! In a passionate embrace she takes him to her body and the evil that has infected her reaches out and embraces Macbeth. Slowly he can feel the demonic possession! He tries to fight it but his wife won't let him think about anything but being king. His good nature tries to fight off the disease that has infected his body but it is a losing battle. The natural evil that exists in all of us (according to the play) has been released and Macbeth prepares to commit the most terrible act anybody in his society can commit, regicide! In one of the most exciting scenes of the play Macbeth sees a floating knife above his head beckoning him to the sleeping chambers of Duncan. The knife seems to be the embodiment of the witches leading him to disaster. At the last minute he can change. At the last minute he can reject evil and opt for goodness. At the last minute he can walk away from everything and keep his immortal soul in tact . . . but he doesn't. In a violent murder he slits the throats of the king and his two grooms, and then smears the blood on the grooms' faces to make it look as if they did the deed. Then Duncan's two sons, afraid that they may be next on the hit parade, blow town leaving guess who to become king. The witches were right. The prophesies all came true (with a little help from a sharp knife) and now the new king and queen can enjoy all the power that they have murdered to get? Or can they? Banquo knows that Macbeth has murdered the king (or at least suspects) and Macbeth knows that Banquo knows. So in order to keep Banquo quiet, Macbeth hires some murderers to cut Banquo's throat. And while they are at it, they might as well cut Banquo's son's throat too so that the prophecy about Banquo's children becoming kings won't come true. Macbeth is basically crazy with evil. First he tries to make a prophecy come true with murder, then he tries to keep a prophecy from happening with murder. The murderers, who are not exactly top draft choices, succeed in butchering Banquo in a terrible fight in the forest but they bungle the murder of Banquo's son. Macbeth begins to worry. What if others suspect that he murdered old Duncan? So he begins a bloody war against citizens of Scotland so that they will know that he and only he is King. But his conscience, or the playfulness of the witches, begin to turn his life into a nightmare. At a big dinner party he sees the ghost of Banquo but nobody else in the room can. He screams and speaks to thin air and acts like a mad man which causes people to doubt that he ought to be king. Anybody who expresses this doubt is butchered. Macbeth really begins to panic and rushes out to that swamp where he first met the witches and asks for help. "Tell me more," he screams. And then, in one of the greatest scenes in Shakespeare, the top witch, Hecate, emerges from Hell. She wants to deal with Macbeth personally. She casts a spell and turns the swamp into a nightmare, a living nightmare, and Macbeth sees visions. Blood flows, lightning flashes, ghostly images walk the swamp and Macbeth is being tortured as if he were living in hell (a little glimpse into his future, actually). During this wild scene Macbeth gets more information. First, he learns that his castle will never fall until the woods around his castle actually uproot themselves and march toward him. Second, he learns that no man born of a woman can ever kill him. Macbeth wakes out of this nightmare with full knowledge that he is invincible. He has absolute power over everybody. So, with this knowledge he spreads his reign of terror even to the strongest nobles that surround him. And the audience watching the show gets a mega dose of Drama that clearly appeals to their moral nature; "If you ask for evil, evil will answer you." The drama will follow Macbeth through the whole play and lead him to destruction.

Meanwhile, there are certain Scotsmen who are plotting against the murderous dictator, as they call him. One of the plotters is Macduff. Macbeth orders the destruction of Macduff's entire household. Macduff hears that every single person in his family, even the livestock, has been butchered. In one of the most dramatic scenes of the play, Macduff swears vengeance against the dictator. Macduff raises an army and a civil war begins. Macbeth has no worry because he knows he cannot die but his wife obviously has some problems. It's as if the evil that floats around only used her to get Macbeth, and as soon as that was accomplished, they left her body because she cannot cope with all the murders and war and she goes mad and then dies. At that point Macbeth speaks one of the most exciting dramas of the play. With all of the death going on around him, his partner of crime gone, and the sound of Macduff's soldiers around his castle, Macbeth says: "What is life, it is a tale told by an idiot full of sound and fury signifying nothing." In an emotional outburst we hear the lines that ell us that this is a lost soul. His life is nothing but a twisted joke devised by the devil. Then all of a sudden the joke gets a little more serious. Somebody reports that the woods around Macbeth's castle are marching! Yes, it is true. Macduff has ordered his soldiers to cut down the limbs of the trees and use them to disguise them from the defenders of the castle. The joke is really on Macbeth. The castle falls. But nobody can seem to kill Macbeth. Remember, he can only be killed by a man not born of woman. Finally Macduff comes face to face with Macbeth and Macbeth warns Macduff that he is invincible. Macduff doesn't care and attacks and, of course, he starts to lose. Macbeth cannot be beaten. At last Macbeth holds the sword high above Macduff and tells him why no man can kill him. And Macduff then closes the trap that brings Macbeth down. Macduff tells him, "I was untimely ripped from my mother's womb." Meaning to the Elizabethans that when Macduff was in his mother's womb, he was ready to be born but his mother couldn't bear him to the world. The unborn child fought and kicked and screamed, and his mother died which threatened the life of the unborn child. So, his father took a knife and slit his dead wife's stomach open and bore the child to life himself. A man bore Macduff, not a woman. Oh, well. Macbeth can't win and he knows it. The witches had tricked him. The promises of the devil are never real. Macduff cuts Macbeth's head off. That's real. With the monster dead Scotland is safe, Macduff is avenged, and the witches have had a pretty good time playing on the earth.

Back in 1606 the audience no doubt went crazy seeing such a show, and so would you if you had seen it presented in such a way as would communicate all of these ideas. Power, violence, action, the supernatural, good vs. evil, demonic possession, demonic practical jokes, sex, suspense, fear, and most of all, a good story which holds your interest until the very end. Now I ask you, could you possibly find all of that boring? Not that it couldn't be made boring by a rotten director and a rotten cast, but if the play is presented with all the right reasons to entertain you, then you will realize that everything you love in action packed films can be found in bigger and better quantities in Shakespeare. Shakespeare only becomes boring when producers try to find some great and overriding aesthetic to communicate rather than the theatrical values that are basic to the plays. Take a chance and see "go for the throat" Shakespeare. If you can't see Shakespeare then see *The Lion King*. Check out the video. You'll see that it is a direct steal from Shakespeare!

Now, what did you learn from *Macbeth?* You ought to have learned the following or else go back to Chapter One and start all over: (1) Shakespeare depended upon exciting plot events to hold his audience's interest. We too are involved in the same kind of plot interest. In Spielberg's *E.T.* we are glued to the screen as the plot unfolds about once every two or three minutes. Spielberg feeds us the plot information slowly but surely until we reach the climax of the film expecting something wonderful to happen to give us a satisfying conclusion to the plot. Consequently, *E.T.* was the most popular film of 1982, even more popular than his other, *Poltergeist. The more satisfying the end of the plot sequence, the more we are pleased with the entertainment.* Remember that. During the same summer as *E.T.* there was a movie called *The Thing.* Both movies dealt with aliens from another planet but both movies did not capture the imagination of the public in the same way. *The Thing* seemed to have all of the elements for good entertainment: story, a good drama, action, the supernatural, etc. However, at the end of the film many of the film's moviegoers felt that they were disappointed in the end of the plot events. You were not sure that the movie was resolved to everybody's satisfaction, or in failing that, resolved to a point that our imaginations were stimulated. *E.T.* on the other hand left everybody in an absolute state of exhilaration. The end of the film was slightly anticipated and definitely accepted. And there was one big difference between the two that we are not going to discuss yet, but that one difference made the film more exciting too. Shakespeare resembles the *E.T.* variety more than *The Thing* type of film. The end of Shakespeare always leaves things clearly explained, figured, and put back together. Even at the end of Macbeth, a play that really deals with the chaos of evil, good is restored in such a way that we are sure that evil has had its day and will not have another because of all the pain that was caused. Nobody at the end of Macbeth can fault Macduff for dispatching Macbeth, and everybody is happy that the son of the old king Duncan is restored to the throne. Also add this idea to your list of items that entertain you. Shakespeare was the first producer of plays who really cared whether or not you really changed your life after seeing his plays, because he decided to take the vary same problems that you had and put them on the stage so that you could see you on stage. Of course he deals with kings and princes and most of you reading this book don't fall into that category, but he also dealt with the common folk. In his play *Henry V,* one of the most exciting war plays ever written, the English army is camped out in France, sick, tired, hungry and completely outnumbered by the French who they have to fight in the morning. Henry, the king, has disguised himself as a knight and has wandered from campfire to campfire trying to test the courage and will of his men. At one particular campfire one of the soldiers curses the king for leading them to die on a battle field where they are sure to go down in defeat, and Henry of course defends the actions of the king pretty well until one little boy pipes out. The kid points out that when it is all over the bodies of the soldiers will be butchered and at last the souls will go to hell, they will be waiting for the king to die. And when the king dies, how will he be able to answer all the accusing ghosts who died needlessly on foreign soil.

Friends, that is exciting stuff. That is the stuff that great playwrights are made of. Shakespeare can deal with the great and the common all in the same play and make them all seem greater than they really are. Shakespeare uplifts the spirit and asks us to be greater than we thought we could be. Shakespeare asks the most difficult questions and offers the most difficult and entertaining answers for our understanding. Now I can hear a lot of you saying, "sure it is exciting stuff if you can understand the language." Of course Shakespeare writes in the contemporary English of the late 16th, early 17th Centuries. So what? Once you begin to listen, it all sounds easy on the ear. Once you forget that "thou" and "thy" are foreign words, then you seem to understand them easily. Of course this form of drama is difficult at first, but once you settle back into the easy rhythms and delightful use of words that only Shakespeare had been able to create, then it is like having opened a window into history and you have all the fun of sticking your head through it and looking around it.

Shakespeare's impact on our world is so great that all authors since must be compared to him. All plays since have been compared to his. All motion pictures today are compared in interest, style and plot to his, but most importantly, Shakespeare taught us how to experience love in theatre. Here it is folks, the item that we can thank Shakespeare for forever: love. Love is the most important aspect of our humanity, and when it is used in either or both the drama and the theatre, the entertainment factor skyrockets. Shakespeare was the first playwright to make us cry for lost love and go crazy for found love. In play after play love becomes his theme, his plot, his character, and his ultimate action. In his play *Romeo and Juliet*, two teenage lovers do everything they can to keep their love from being crushed by unfeeling and uncaring adults. At last in their frustration they run away, get married, and try to spring for freedom but in the process they both die. They needlessly die because the adults are so angry and so obstinate in their ways. At the end of the play everybody realizes that a little bit of love from both of the families could have avoided the tragedies of their deaths. In *Hamlet* a boy so loves his father and is so disappointed in his mother's love for his father that he takes up vengeance against the people who murdered his father. In *Henry IV* Pt. One, Henry Bolingbroke is so crushed by his son's lack of love for him that he nearly goes crazy. In one of the most tender and beautiful scenes ever written, Prince Hal tells his father that he loves him and hithermore will be his son. In *Henry IV* Pt. Two old Falstaff loves his former playmate, King Henry. Since the king rejects him, Falstaff dies for want of him. And the list goes on and on. Shakespeare knew that mixed with that strange nature in the human spirit that revels in violence and death, there is also that need that wants love and all the problems that come from loving another person. In the long run, love makes us feel good, feel bad, feel excited, but most of all it makes us FEEL. It cannot be denied and it cannot be defeated. *E.T.* might go down in film history as one of the most exciting movies ever produced. Why? Well, we discussed in part what makes it successful but I think its greatest attraction is love. It's basically the love story of a little boy and an alien. The little boy loves the alien so much that he nearly dies for him and the alien loves the little boy so much that he nearly dies for him. All in all the audience develops such a love for both of them that they forget how much hate they carry for other things in their lives. The movie is so loving that it makes you love a bit of plastic and metal as if it is a human being. The movie strikes such a gentle note in us that for a brief moment we can forget the cruelty of the world, the futility of our lives and the meaninglessness of hate. And for all of this we can thank William Shakespeare.

Before we leave Shakespeare I want to deal with another one of his plays which I think will also make a pretty good impact on you. Most of us enjoy watching movies and plays about people with human and identifiable flaws. Remember that word *vicarious*? Well, when you see a person who has the same problems that you have you tend to understand and appreciate the character much more because you identify with the character. Shakespeare was the first playwright who successfully brought the noble person with the serious character flaw to the modern stage. Now I know that none of you reading this book have any character flaws in you at all, but aren't you a little interested in those characters you see on screen who have just a little bit of problem dealing with life? The whole success of James Dean, the rebel without a cause, Marlon Brando's character in *On The Waterfront,* and even the central character in the TV series, *The Greatest American Hero,* are characters who never seem to cope well with life even through we want them to succeed. Richie Cunningham in *Happy Days* is such a character. Well, they all go back to one of the most controversial, unhappy, bumbling, sometimes heroic, and definitely interesting characters; Hamlet. God, stop saying to yourself, "I don't want to hear about Hamlet!" Yes, you do. You'll want to hear about Shakespeare's Hamlet, not what Hamlet has developed into down through the ages. Hamlet is really the first modern play that tried to give man a real choice to be a vengeful animal or a rational seeker of justice. Almost every cop show you see on TV has some of it. *N.Y.P.D. Blue,* a current TV hit, has the most of *Hamlet* of anything on TV today. So what is *Hamlet* and why is *Hamlet?* What it is is a play about a man who must seek revenge for his father's murder. Why is Hamlet, because there is nobody else in Hamlet's world who cares about justice. The play begins with the news that a ghost (remember, Shakespeare knew his audience) has been seen walking about the ramparts of a castle in Denmark. The inhabitants of the castle are not scared since there has been no proof that anybody of worth has really seen the ghost. And then Hamlet sees the ghost. The ghost is the ghost of his own father who everybody knows was murdered. But nobody knows who the murderer(s) were. The ghost tells all. It tells Hamlet that Hamlet's mother and his uncle killed him by pouring poison in his ear while he slept in a garden. Hamlet can't believe that his own mother murdered his father, her husband, but a ghost doesn't lie (I've known some who have but they weren't kings of Denmark). Hamlet begs his father for instruction and the ghost simply says, take vengeance. Vengeance means kill those who killed your kin. O.K., what does Hamlet do? He got it right from the ghost's mouth. He has the right to pick up a knife and kill. But does he? Does he avenge murder? No. He thinks. He tries to understand why his world has been turned upside down. The answers are not easy. Now I know you might have heard that such actors as Mel Gibson and Richard Burton have played Hamlet. And these were good looking, strong men who made Hamlet a hero but that is bullpucky. Hamlet is a dope. Or at least as much a dope as some of us are. First, his father was killed with little or no thought that his son might be strong enough to take vengeance if he found out. Second, he has been at school for a long time! He is in his early thirties and yet he is still going to college in Germany when most boys had finished their education by their late teens? Why? Is Hamlet stupid? Probably not. Is Hamlet just not ready to meet life? Probably so. Like most of us it is hard to think of taking responsibility in this wild and jungle-like world. Hamlet is not ready to take on any responsibility. He probably drinks too much and eats too much. Many times in the play we get hints that he is overweight. So, this poor dope who is not emotionally or physically ready to avenge his father and take over the job of a king has to get himself ready immediately.

First, he decides to pretend to be crazy so that the royal household won't suspect him of being a real threat to the throne (although there is no evidence that anybody thinks that he is a threat to do anything). The acting job really hurts his fiancee who loves him but Hamlet, a rather selfish guy, really doesn't care about her anymore although there is evidence at the end of the play that he had seduced her and had made love to her with the promise of marriage. Maybe he is planning on catching the murderers and then marrying her? Or perhaps he thinks that maybe she had something to do with the murder? At any rate his stupid pretense that he is mad causes everybody to suspect him of something although nobody knows exactly what he is up to and Hamlet doesn't even know what he is up to. Finally, the king, the queen and the prime minister set a trap for Hamlet to see if he is really as mad as he is supposed to be and Hamlet carries off his mad act perfectly. But then in a scene with his mother, with the prime minister hiding in a closet, Hamlet, who is trying to tell his mother that he knows about her crime, accidentally kills the prime minister, whom he thinks is the king. When he discovers that he killed the wrong man he doesn't even seem sorry. Maybe he is going crazy. He just killed the prime minister, who by the way was going to be his future father-in-law, and he doesn't even shed a tear. There is a good reason to believe that this is the first time he ever harmed anybody in his life and he seems to show no remorse. What kind of man is this anyway? A very interesting one, actually.

Well, the murder of the prime minister is treated as an act of a mad man, and Hamlet is not punished for it so he is free to try another way to bring justice to the front. Hamlet hires a bunch of actors and instructs them in a brand new play. He shows them how to act out the murder of the old king. Then he arranges a party and asks the new king and the queen to watch the performance, and then Hamlet watches the king to see if he will crack. The king cracks all right and stops the play but what does Hamlet do? Does he do anything? Nope. He just can't make up his mind what to do. He is scared. He is confused. Should he take vengeance and put to rest the poor soul of the king, or should he wait and let God punish this man after he dies for surely he would go to hell for his crimes? He makes up his mind to take vengeance. He picks up a knife and sets out to find the king. He finds him praying. Hamlet stops and watches and listens. The king asks forgiveness for his crimes as he confesses them. Hamlet is shocked. He can't kill a man while he is in a state of confession because, he reasons, his soul would go to heaven. Again Hamlet rationalizes his way out of doing what he is supposed to do. Does all of this sound familiar to you? I don't mean the idea of taking blood vengeance on people. Doesn't this idea of always rationalizing what you should do and what you shouldn't do seem familiar? You do it. Hamlet does it so perhaps there is a little Hamlet in all of us. One of the ways of recognizing what we are is by watching somebody on stage who has our faults act them out. Right?

Now, back to Hamlet. He's in big trouble in the play because the king decides he could be trouble and plans to have him murdered. Hamlet, who has a wonderful sense of self preservation at this time, doesn't fall for the clumsy trap that is set for him but runs away instead. Meanwhile his fiancee commits suicide, another tragedy in his life. Hamlet returns to be at the funeral and ends up having a verbal fight with his dead fiancee's brother. The fight results in a challenge to a duel which Hamlet accepts. The king plots to have a poison sword slipped into the duel so that Hamlet will be killed even if he is only scratched. The duel takes place, the sword not only kills Hamlet but it also kills his once future brother-in-law. In the big conclusion, the king dies and the queen dies too. Hamlet has revenged his father's murder and managed to get himself killed too. Seems silly and wasted doesn't it yet there is a wonderful piece of theatre here. We are rather vengeful people, right? If someone cuts in front of you in a car, you can't wait childishly to cut back in front of him. If somebody flips you off you naturally flip him off. Vengeance is sweet we are told. Shakespeare tells us that it may be sweet but it is also deadly. In the movies we love to see revenge. In Clint Eastwood's old Italian westerns the man with no name was always getting even with somebody and when he did we felt satisfaction, *vicariously*. Shakespeare knew that his audience loved vengeance too but he also knew that what they should love is love, not vengeance. By making vengeance very exciting but not rewarding he accomplished the tasks of both entertaining and teaching: Theatre, and Drama, respectively.

After all of this you've got to love Shakespeare. If you don't, then do as I suggested and see him done with emotion and guts! See Shakespeare performed as sheer theatrical entertainment and the genius of the play will enter your brain through the emotions. *Remember:* we are not intellectuals. We are feeling emotional creatures who respond with our emotions, not our brains. Shakespeare knew that he wrote beautiful poetry, but the poetry is based solidly in ego, violence, love, hate, revenge, sympathy, empathy, tenderness, and powerful action. The intellectual use of words is only a wonderful by-product of his wonderfully crafted emotional stories. And these stories were acted only by men? No women at all!

The Elizabethan period enjoyed Shakespeare's plays because Queen Elizabeth loved the theatre. In 1603 she died and although theatre didn't die it certainly took a shot to the tummy when the next king, James I, became king. Most of you know the name from the Bible that he had translated but most of you didn't know that this ignominious rolly eyed, ego centered, pseudo-intellectual helped create a form of theatre that not only we enjoy but are victimized by at the same time. I don't like James I. He had a lot of problems and none of them were good for England. He wasn't a man of the people. He didn't think that above all he was English, as the old queen had thought. Basically he was not a likable person, not to mention being an inept ruler.

CHAPTER 5

Tear-out Study Guide

1. Elizabethans took their name from _____.

2. Bravado means _____.

3. The Elizabethans were the perfect combination of _____ and _____ values.

4. Shakespeare became one of the western world's greatest _____.

5. What is the Drama of Macbeth? _____.

6. Shakespeare knew how to scare his audience using _____ and _____.

7. In 1588 the English defeated the _____.

8. Only _____ performed Shakespeare's plays.

9. What did manifest destiny mean to the Elizabethans? _____.

10. One of the reasons Shakespeare's plays were so successful was because Queen Elizabeth _____.

Jacobean Theatre and Drama

James Stuart, king of England. James means "Jacobean." He was a skeptical person who didn't trust many people above all honest people. He was an international joke who brought more dishonor to the throne than he did honor. Consequently, the image of the Englishman, at least his foreign image, began to suffer. If you have trouble getting a picture of what the man looked like, then think of Ross Perot who also thought he was the Pope and you'll nail him perfectly.

What happened to theatre and what kind of theatre became popular was really determined by what happened to the English personality at this time. While Shakespeare loved to write about high adventure in a land far, far away, ala *Star Wars,* it only worked while the Englishman was in a mood to escape reality. After 1603 the Englishman was too concerned with the nasty reality that he was living in a bad time, and a playwright named Ben Jonson helped him see reality in a nasty way. Ben Jonson is the playwright who first realized that there was a sucker born every minute. His view of life, formed by what he saw, was that man was basically dishonest and would cheat you if he could. Helped along with the era of James I, he wrote plays which told us that you had better keep your hand on your wallet when you walk down the street or somebody else will keep his hand on your wallet. Interestingly enough, Ben Jonson really scored very well. In fact he became the most popular playwright of the time. And you know, there is something in us that really is attracted to the ideas of Ben Jonson too. If you've seen a picture called *The Sting,* and how popular it was, then you have some idea how popular Ben Jonson was. In *The Sting,* you had a basic scam executed perfectly in order to fool, trick, and swindle somebody out of cash. We're all really attracted to the idea that somebody trying to get something for nothing ought to get burned for being greedy. Nobody can cheat an honest man but trying to find an honest man is more than a difficult task. Ben Jonson felt that there were no honest men. Given the opportunity, says Jonson, every person will put honesty and morality to one side in favor of the scam. Pretty cynical? Yes, but also probably right, too. Shakespeare didn't believe this and Elizabeth didn't believe this but perhaps they were just too child-like in their world view of the harsh world. It all depends on what you think the world is like. Certainly greed is a powerful force and one that entertains us a great deal. I would like to coin the term, "Jonsonize" in honor of the great Ben Jonson. Jonsonize means to fool us and trick us. You get Jonsonized when you see an ad in the paper that says genuine diamond ring for sale. Just send $10.00 bucks and get a "real" diamond ring. You get all excited and send the money; eighteen weeks later you get a small stapled bag in the mail containing your genuine diamond ring. The only thing diamond about this ring is the shape of the glass. Did you really expect to get a diamond ring in the mail for only $10.00? You're crazy. You were an open target for Jonsonizing. If we put that on film, I mean if we filmed your whole experience, from the time you opened the paper and saw the ad to the time you got the whole idea for sending away until the time we saw your face when you opened the package and saw your ring, it would make an interesting picture. Why? Because something in us loves to see somebody else get cheated as long as we aren't the ones. That's right. You love to see somebody else experience the pain of losing but you don't like to lose. Ben Jonson knew that there was a fool born every day! We all love scams. *The Flim Flam Man* was a movie made several years ago which showed what happened when a man, offering a quick way to limited wealth, turned himself loose on a southern community. The results? He became rich while they became poor, and never once did he lie to them about what they were doing or what they could expect to get. Do you like films about gambling? Of course you do because there is excitement in watching somebody trying to beat the odds. There is something exciting about watching somebody throwing 7 after 7 on the dice tables even though in the end this person can't win. You pull for him to break the house; you hope that he can beat the odds. I guess it is part of our need to see the underdog win coupled with the idea that in no way can an honest person really get something for nothing. The whole idea is really complex and it touches the most exciting and interesting part of our psyche; we love to see somebody lose at the same time beat the establishment. Let me give you another example through a true story.

The other day (about two years ago) I was sitting home reading a book, nice and comfortable, when all of a sudden I heard my mail box. "Great," I said, "the mail always brings interesting stuff." In the mail was a letter that said, "Important." I was impressed. "Open at once" the envelope commanded. I did. The first thing I saw inside was a picture of a Rolls Royce. I got excited. Then I saw a picture of a big house on Long Island. Oh boy. Then I saw a picture of a pile of cash, fifty thousand bucks! Lord. And then I saw a picture of a big question mark which was bigger than all of the other pictures. Fantastic! The letter read as follows; "Congratulations! Your name has been specially selected by a computer process. This is a promotional stunt designed to help us sell a product and you, you lucky guy, have been selected to win big so that we can advertise big!" I went out of my mind. I was going to get something for free! I was going to get a car, or a house, or cash, or who knows? Maybe I was going to get everything!!! I read on. "In order to collect your prize, hurry down to the address printed at the bottom of the page and collect your prize." I was trembling. I looked down and spotted the address. It was a little office building down on the main street of town. The office building normally handled massage parlors, showrooms for discontinued motel color TVs, and returned motel furniture. I jumped in my car and drove downtown. It was 101 degrees that day and my air conditioner wasn't working but I didn't care; nobody sweats in a Rolls Royce. The steering wheel was so hot that it burned my hands but I didn't care. I was one of the lucky chosen! Now I knew how rich people felt just before they went to the bank. There was no place to park in front of the office building so I parked in a red zone. No problem, it wouldn't take long to stuff my money in the shopping bag I had brought along. I got out of the car and hurried upstairs. Rm 309. I stopped in front of the door. My heart was beating so fast I figured I would pass out before I'd get to collect my house. I knocked. I could hear footsteps coming to the door. The door swung open and there standing before me was a man about five foot 8 inches, 220 lbs., sweaty off-white shirt with big stains under his arms, his tie askew, his zipper half down, his face wet, and the five o'clock shadow had started at about two in the afternoon. I said, "I've come for my Rolls." He looked at me and frowned. I showed him my letter. A big smile oozed across his face and he said, "this way." I walked through the door. I wondered where they were keeping my car? The office was about twelve feet by twelve feet with beer cans littered all over the place. No matter what I saw, my *anticipation* was so strong that I simply said to myself, "Look, if they're giving away Rolls Royces and houses they can't spend money on fancy offices." All over the walls of the office were pretty pictures, all framed. Pictures of smiling girls smelling flowers, I figured that they were past winners.

"Sit down, fella," the sweaty angel of fortune said. "I'd like the Rolls," I said. "Sure, you would, but there's a little business we have to do first." I should have known there was really something wrong here when he took out this big photo album of pictures and said, "Look, before we get to the prizes, I'm supposed to tell you about this neat photo process that you can buy at a discount." I have to admit my heart bounced a little, I knew there was more to this lucky stroke of good luck than met the eye, but I had my heart set on a car. "Photo process?" I said. "Yeah, it won't take long and then I can get to your prizes." My heart leaped again. I knew it. I was on the up and up. I was going to get my prizes. For one hour and a half I sat there listening to him drone on about this process and that process, always telling me that the company that was providing all of the great prizes was the best photo film and process company in the world. It was hot in the office and I was getting a little dizzy and a little thirsty and I really wanted to get out of there, but I wasn't going to leave without my car, or the house, or even the money, and then there was that big question mark which probably meant I would get them all. I sat. At last he was finished. He leaned over the table and said, "Well, how about it?" "How about what?" I asked. "Do you want to buy a photo album?" "No," I said. The guy's face clouded up. "Didn't you hear what I was reading?" "Yeah, but I don't have a camera," I lied. He smiled. "O.K., no sweat, we'll fix that." There must be a camera in the glove compartment of the Rolls, I thought. He disappeared into a closet and then came out with a big game board. He set it up right in front of me. Along the top it said, Be a Winner! A Prize Behind Every Square! My heart started beating again. The fat sweaty man took my letter, stamped it with some very official looking stamps and then smiled. "You ready?" I nodded. He handed me a pin and said, "Behind every square there is a prize. Punch out the square and you"ll get a prize." I looked at the pin. Incredible. One little two inch pin was the key to my good luck. I looked at the board. No hint to where the Rolls was, but gee, it didn't make any difference. I plunged the pin into the center. I pulled the pin out and there revealed before me was the "Question Mark." The fat man looked at me and smiled, "Boy you must have been born under a lucky star." My heart beat faster. "You got the best prize of all!" I knew it! I was going to get all of the prizes. He withdrew a letter from his drawer with a big "?" on it. "Open this letter, boy, and smile." I ripped the letter open and out fell a note. With trembling hands I picked it up and read it. "Congratulations, big winner! You have won the most valuable gift we can give. Get ready . . . you have won . . . six months of free photo processing." I stared at the letter. The fat man was talking to me. "Boy are you lucky. Because you won the prize I can make you the following offer. If you buy $600.00 worth of film I can give you a 30% discount right now so that you can really take advantage of your great prize." I stared at him. "Where's my car?" "And I can also give you a great discount," he reached into a drawer, "on this great little camera that normally sells for about $69.00 but you get for $49.00!" I stared at him. "What about my house, my money?" "The total bill comes to $449.00. Cash? Or do you want to put it on your credit card?" I got up. The fat man was yelling something at me. "Hey, don't you want your prize?" I got into the oven and drove home. On the way I thought to myself, JONSONIZED.

Is that clear? Why are we such suckers? And why do we love to watch people get suckered? Because, we are all greedy and we all love to see greed punished or rewarded. When it is punished we get comedy and when it is rewarded we feel exhilarated. At the end of *The Sting* we cheer the swindlers because they were smart enough to pull off the big scam. But when we see Lucy end up with 800 lbs of frozen food that she can't use we scream with laughter. Ben Jonson was called a writer of comedies because his plays were exactly what people wanted to laugh at. One of his best plays is called *The Alchemist.* It's about a fellow who lives in London and works as a servant. When the master goes off on vacation the servant turns the master's house into a scam palace. There is a fortune teller in one room, a fake jewel dealer in another. And in one of the rooms is a man who claims that he can turn base metal into gold. Of course everybody in the play cheats everybody else and in the end the cheaters get caught. They don't get punished but they get caught. Interesting that Ben Jonson won't allow his swindlers in the play to be punished. Perhaps he thought the audience was on the side of the cheaters. He was right. His other play that is really worth talking about is called *Volpone,* the fox. An old man spreads the word to all his friends and relatives that he is dying. Of course most of his relatives think the old man is rich so they come to his deathbed in order to make sure that they are in the will. Most of them find out that they may or may not be named out, if certain "favors" are given him, the relative's name will be mentioned. Of course, the whole thing is a scam, a trick, just to entertain Volpone. However, the play begins to become really interesting when Volpone decides that he needs the favors of the wife of one of his cousins. He convinces the greedy cousin that it would be a wonderful gesture to allow his wife to crawl into bed with him just to give a few of his remaining moments of life some satisfaction. In turn, Volpone says that he would be very "grateful" to his cousin. His cousin can't resist the opportunity to be included in the will and so he forces his wife to keep the old man company. Now the wife wants no part of the whole thing but because her husband's greed is so strong she ends up being a sacrifice. Her husband rationalizes by suggesting that a dying old man couldn't do anything physical to her. He claims that all she has to do is lie by him in bed and give him a few moments of pleasure. Does the husband really think that Volpone won't try to have intercourse with her? It doesn't make any difference what he believes because his goal is to get into the will any way he can.

Well, the evening comes and the young wife is standing in front of the bed and Volpone is practically drooling. She suspects that perhaps he isn't as close to death as everybody assumes but nevertheless she does climb into bed with him. What then happens is the typical action of a man who enjoys a practical joke. Volpone suddenly comes to life and the wife realizes that she is in bed with a rather virile old man who is bent on having his way with the lady. She allows it to go close to rape and then runs out of bed screaming right to the police. Volpone is arrested and charged with several crimes including attempted rape. At the conclusion of the play Volpone is found guilty and punished.

The play itself is very funny and filled with wonderful characterizations but what makes the play really exciting for us is that the work that Ben Jonson does in the play is really very cynical. And for some strange reason we love to watch cynical people get punished. I guess we feel that a person who expects the worst and then gets the worst is really funny.

Ben Jonson was a favorite of King James because down deep in his soul he really enjoyed the use of tricks, scams, and jokes to make asses out of people. In some ways that is exactly how he ran his government. Not only did James like Ben Jonson's plays but he also loved Jonson's masques. A masque is a kind of nightclub performance featuring poetry, music, dancing given privately and only once for the appreciation of some important people. Actually, the masque was the forerunner of the Las Vegas nightclub or casino show of today. Fancy costumes, beautiful women and good looking men, music, etc. all theatrically make up the masque. And although we don't use the poem or Greek myth as drama for the theatre as Ben Jonson did, the pop song serves the same purpose. If you like to sit in a lounge, sip a beverage, look at beautiful ladies parading around in practically nothing and listen to a comic or a singer performing at the same time then you and James I would probably get along pretty well. We really don't need to spend much more time on this masque business because its importance to us is relatively slight. What is more interesting is what the attitude of the people were when they realized that their king was more interested in private shows than in public shows. I believe that the country, especially those Englishmen who lived in London, began to feel as if they were leaderless. Slowly the attitude of the people began to turn inward. People began attending plays that not only didn't celebrate life, as Shakespeare's plays had tried to do, but made a point of celebrating death. A playwright named John Webster wrote a play called *The Duchess of Malfi* at this time which examined the dark motivations of a disturbed murderer. The play was so popular that it made Webster a very popular fellow and it also indicated that the English were becoming very interested in the perverted actions of a homicidal maniac. From *The Duchess of Malfi* we get movies like the *Fan, Halloween,* and *In The Mouth of Madness* and others which exploit psychological perversion. These movies are popular. Let's face it, most of you screamed your way through *Halloween* and enjoyed it. Interestingly enough, most of these kinds of movies and plays become popular when governments begin to erode. Is this a sign of our times? Do we go into horror films and pretend that our government leaders are the ones getting axed to death? Probably not, but it is peculiar that when times get bad the movies and plays look for the worst, and it is also interesting that when times begin to get better horror films tend to be less popular, and high romance films and plays become very popular. Today, both horror films and high romance films are popular. We're really mixed up. Well, King James wasn't mixed up because he thought that he was "the left hand of God" and, therefore, he couldn't be fooled by anybody . . . unless God made a fool of him!

One last gift from the Ben Jonson legacy is something we enjoy more and more, today. In fact we might love it even more than the Jacobeans did. It's called Satire. So, what is satire? It means poking fun at something serious. We're really good at that nowadays. We don't treat too many things or people or even presidents too seriously. We can always find something to ridicule. I think we are too cynical and the more cynical we become the more we deal in satire. *Saturday Night Live* is the best example of satire that I know. Nothing is sacred on that show. Nothing is safe from the biting wit of plain old subtle punch in the face comedy that the SNL crowd is famous for delivering. We see satire in all forms today. Political cartoons, comic books, TV shows and of course movies. Woody Allen is a satirist . . . most of the time he's making fun of Pseudo-intellectuals who take themselves too seriously. Ben Jonson liked to satirize greedy people. Do you remember the Monty Python crowd? If not get yourself to a video store and get some of their films. Better yet get some of their TV shows. Wonderfully funny and filled with satire. Benny Hill. Same thing. Good satire makes you laugh. Bad satire makes you wonder what all the fuss is about. Good satire makes you think of the subject of satire in a new way. Bad satire doesn't make you think at all. So, if you haven't figured it out yet, *satire is a form of drama.* I say a form of drama because it also inspires the theatrical element of laughter. But basically, satire tries to make you think. Most of the time satire attacks bigshots. President Clinton suffers a lot of ridicule from Rush Limbaugh. That's o.k. because Limbaugh is an entertainer and he finds a lot to satirize in Clinton. Clinton finds a lot to satirize in Limbaugh as well! If you're not important then there is nothing to satirize. Ross Perot is ready made for satire. He sticks his personality out there like a target: hit me! So, what films have scored the most with satire. I think films like *Airplane, Airplane II, Police Story, Naked Gun* are pretty good examples of poking fun at serious adventure movies.

So, Ben Jonson looked at his society and found much to ridicule . . . although he had to be careful. Satirize the wrong person in those days and you could lose more than your reputation!

In 1625 Holy King James I died. And his son King Charles I took the throne. Charles was an egomaniac, a fool, and a bungler. Other than that he was a great king . . . not! He spent a lot of money trying to defeat Scotland in war and he had absolutely no idea what his subjects felt about life, England and the pursuit of happiness. Afterall, he was the "left hand of God" and could do no wrong! But "lefty" made some terrible mistakes! And these mistakes would eventually keep him from getting ahead in this world.

For the next thirty years things in England declined so much that a new political party, the Puritans, wanted some big changes. On the other hand, the King of England felt that the country was not responding to the Divine Right Of Godly Appointed Kings. The result was a bloody civil war which began in 1642 and lasted until 1648. During that time the power struggle between Roundheads (as the Puritans were called) and the Cavaliers (as the soldiers loyal to King Charles I were called) succeeded in destroying all the theaters in London, throwing the country into chaos, and nearly ruining the entire economy of the nation. At the conclusion of the war, Charles I found himself arrested by the Puritans and charged with treason against the state. If this were a history book only, the trial of Charles I would make a great class. It was dramatic, original, politically incredible, and definitely theatrical. But since this isn't a history book, suffice to say: they cut his head off. Never before in England had anything like this happened and never again would it happen. Although a lot of English would like to see current Prince Charles lose his head. Anyway, the Puritans hated theatre and so for the next ten years theaters in London were parking lots!

This doesn't mean that there wasn't good theatre going on in the rest of Europe. France was producing a great deal for a selected audience and so was Italy, but in my opinion none of the work at that time had any real effect on what we appreciate in theatre today. I think we have to go back to England ten years later. In 1660 the British Parliament asked Charles' son, Charles II, to return to London and take the throne. Charles accepted and he was restored.

Charles Stuart II was a fantastic man. When the civil war started he was just a kid but by the end of it he was leading men into battle (not very successfully though). Before his father had his head cut off, Charles II had barely escaped England with his life. He had to resort to disguise and quick thought to escape with his life. When he got to the Continent he found that Cromwell (the dictator who took over after the King Dictator was executed) had set a price on his head. Even the British secret service was hot on his trail. For ten years he raced around Europe trying to keep from getting killed and trying to enlist the aid of his fellow kings and queens. There are lots of stories about the wandering Charlie Stuart. Most of them are super pieces of theatre and have made great movies. One such story has it that Charles had been trapped in a windmill in Flanders. Several, maybe as many as twelve of Cromwell's black robed secret service, armed with pistol and sword raced into the windmill after the fleeing Charles. Citizens around the windmill heard shot after shot and the clanging of steel. Finally, Charles Stuart stepped out of the windmill, his clothes torn, bleeding from several wounds. He climbed upon his horse and rode away. Curious citizens peeked inside the windmill to witness the bodies of all the secret service men. Now whether or not that story was true, we don't know but it did serve to romanticize the legend of Charles Stuart the exiled king. We do know that Charles became a lean crafty and very dangerous man. He loved women, lots of women. He loved hard drink and hard living. And most of all he loved all of his vices at one time while he was watching the theatre. Yes, he loved the stage. When he was restored to the throne, he set about changing the public's mind about a lot of things.

CHAPTER 6

Tear-out Study Guide

1. Jacobean means _____.

2. The King thought he was the left hand of _____.

3. Ben Jonson was a famous _____.

4. Ben Jonson knew that there was a fool _____.

5. "Jonsonized" means _____.

6. *Volpone* was a good example of the Jacobean attitude because most of the characters were_____.

7. A masque is _____.

8. John Webster wrote a play called _____.

9. Satire means _____.

10. *Saturday Night Live* is an example of _____.

Restoration Theatre
Is the Name of the Game

When Charles II rode back into London at the head of his victorious court in exile, he must have enjoyed the irony of a king who had to sneak out of England only ten years before coming back ten years later with the entire country at his feet, not to mention several heads of men who had tried to kill him when he was running for his life in Europe. What he found in London when he returned was pretty boring. First, the theatres had been all closed. Second, the Puritan influence had caused life in London to be pretty plain. Charles was used to a rather wild life in Europe and he didn't plan to change. Instead he set the standard for London to change. The first thing Charles did was to Frenchify London. The meant that he wanted a certain style set for the city which would eventually be call Restoration Fashion. Even Charles didn't figure how out of control it would all get. First, you have to realize that most people living in London hated the Puritan element that had been running the country for the past ten years. A great many of the London folk, especially the young ones, wanted a taste of the good European life that they had been reading about. The more the young nobles and people of some wealth wanted to rebel against the Puritan ethic, the tighter the rules became. So, when Charles returned, he returned to a city that had been stretched like a rubber band just waiting for an excuse to snap back far in the other direction. The restoration of the king was the perfect excuse. What happened to London is even hard to imagine, let alone describe. London became more Rome than Caligula's Rome. It became more Paris than Louis XIV's Paris. Licentious only describes part of what the city became. Lewd, disgusting, lascivious, brutal, lawless and insulting describes it a bit better. Of all the elements of theatre that fit the style of the period, *sex* seems to be the most appropriate description. Within a few years all moral standards disappeared, the family unit began to break down, marriage became a social joke, gin, and other hard drinks became so popular that the entire city seemed to be given over to madness. Opiates and dangerous drugs flourished in every corner of London. The entire moral fabric of the city started to unravel. And all of this was a direct backlash to the strict control of the Puritan element. It is out of this period that we get the modern pornography that has become so economically successful in America today. Sex and the exploitation of sex made the Restoration period a very wild place to live and *Deep Throat* the biggest money maker in modern film history.

First, let us examine this whole business of sex in the movies and in plays. Remember, we talked about the vicarious experience of watching a pair of attractive people making love on the screen and then pretending you're up there too. Well, if you think about it that can become a very exciting psychological release for a great many people. It can also be a very dangerous motivation for such people as John Hinkley who sees more of Jody Foster on the screen than most people do. But for some strange reason we all love to watch two people making love on the screen. We also feel embarrassed if there are people around watching us watch two people make love. It is tough to go to a steamy love picture with parents. We wonder if they wonder about you making love with somebody. And after all, love making is a private business; that's why we go to the movies to see it. In the dark movie theatre or playhouse we sit and watch that which we are not supposed to see. It is partaking of the forbidden fruit that makes sex on the screen so exciting. Even TV cable channels sex "after hours" for the viewer who wants to stay up late in the night to enjoy the sights of breast and thigh locked in a sweaty embrace. The TV cable people even take pains to tell us that the sexy movies will only be shown at *night* as if nighttime were some magic time reserved for sex. At any rate, sex is entertaining and that is what this book is all about: the study of what entertains. Restoration people thought sex was so entertaining that they devoted every waking moment of their lives for one whole generation to it. But the sex that was popular in the Restoration period was illicit sex, stolen sex, sex with another man's wife or another wife's husband. Sex in the ordinary way smacked of procreation, not entertainment, and the Restoration types were not interested in anything as mundane as ordinary sex. Sex for them had to be part of a plot to embarrass somebody or trick somebody out of something. Let's take a look at some of the plays of the period and discover if there are any characteristics that are prevalent today (you know there will be!)

A dapper fellow named Wycherly wrote a play called *The Country Wife* at this time which goes like this: a fellow named Horner (figured him out yet?) spreads the word that he has just come back from Europe with a disease which has left him totally helpless when it comes to dealing with women. Or in other words, the man is too limp to love. The husbands of all his friends, who are always trying to catch their wives in romantic situations, decide that Horner is the perfect man to watch over all the women. What they don't know is that the guy has been lying and he is as straight and ready to go as an Amtrak Train heading into a tunnel. He has found a way to get all the women he can handle (and he manages to handle all of them) without worrying about the husbands. Well, one old man finds himself a young little girl in the country, marries her, and then takes her to London. Naturally, he begins to worry about all the rascals in London who would like to take her to bed, and while he is worrying about the men he forgets to "take care of his wife" who begins to look around for herself. Naturally, she finds Horner who also finds her, and after they find each other she finds that her husband needs to either be younger or less jealous of her relationship with the world. The whole play is an excuse to have some nasty fun, put down the other generation, and poke fun at country life. The art of sexual "put-down" really came into its own at this time and the Restoration audiences seemed to love laughing at somebody's sexual inferiority. Very typical of that idea was a not very successful movie called *Porky's*. *Porky's* is a perfect example of Restoration theatre at its worst. It takes a social group, explores its perverted sexual nature, takes stupid potshots at sexual taboos, and provides you with absolutely nothing but juvenile laughs. The Restoration period even gave us some role models for soap opera since it was obsessed by the idea that gossip was more important than conversation and treachery is more interesting than heroics. I think it is interesting to note that in Restoration Drama there are no heroes! Right, you can't find a single person who we would say is a hero. Certainly Horner is funny and kind of a stud but is that a hero? To the Restoration types he was, but to us he really is just a horny guy who is trying to get a little. Take a look at *Saturday Night Fever, Grease,* or any of the movies that have told us that being a good lover or a sexy lover is better than being a good person or a righteous person, and then I think you have a good idea of what that kind of theatre was like three hundred years ago and why the remnants of it are still hanging around. Remember this: when a period of theatre produces theatre without a traditional hero then there is probably something very wrong with the government or the society or both. Listen to some of the titles of the plays during this period: *Love in a Tub, She Would If She Could, Everybody's Whore, A Short Wick Light No Flame.*

O.K., you're convinced the plays are sexy but so what? There are a lot of sexy plays and movies today that are perverted so what is the big deal? The big deal has to do with sex and society. Child pornography that actually sells indicates that we are in a society that is so curious that it will embarrass itself by looking at something that is disgusting just to relieve the boredom of living. I'm not saying that those of you who watch pornography are pornographic. I'm saying that when a society reaches the point that it has nothing to uplift it, no heroes, no successes, no ideals, then it will look inward and try to explore its worst parts in order to understand itself. So was it with the Restoration period; so is it with us today. Let's take a walk down a street in London on our way to the theatre and try to picture why this society had turned so bad.

It is about three in the afternoon. It is very important that we go to the theatre early because at night there are so many thugs and cutthroats on the streets that if we stay out really late there is a chance we will never get home. As we stroll down the street we see a typical lady of fashion coming to us. Actually we can probably smell her before we see her since the Restoration man and woman seldom bathed. They simply used heavy perfumes to cover up the smells. What a vision of beauty with her wig piled up on her head. Most of these wigs were actually orphanages for assorted fleas and lice. She probably was wearing a fine silk or fine cotton dress which she rarely changed. The dress was designed to show off the figure and many of the ladies exposed their breasts which were decorated by beauty marks. She had just made up her face. It was popular then to cover one's face with a lead based makeup which hardened like plaster and it cracked when you smiled.

The lead based makeup caused a great deal of cancer but that was no problem. If you noticed a hole in your face or a pock mark from a bout with the plague you just covered it up with a beauty mark (beauty?). Some ladies had a measles of beauty marks. It was popular to smear colors on the lips and cheeks (any colors). There was an 80% chance that if the lady were popular among the men that she had V.D. If she were accompanied by a "gentleman," he might have looked like this. He was also wearing a wig and like the lady he had shaved his head the morning before to give his scalp a little chance to get some air. He was probably wearing silks also. If he were a daring fellow there would probably be no crotch to the silks. He was constantly taking some foreign substance up to his nose and inhaling it. Some of you think that it was snuff, but in reality there was a pretty good chance that it was a strong narcotic. In his right hand he had a long walking cane which could have had a sword in it, or the top of it was made of a hard substance for defending himself in a brawl. His favorite drink was probably the newly invented gin, which was little better than straight poison. The cases of liver disease rose remarkably during this period. On the streets around us we might see little children dead or dying from drinking too much because there was no legal age for drinking at this time. Also, because the plague was unchecked at this time, we might have to step over bodies that had not been cleaned up. Down the street we see a band of young men around twenty years old who are dressed well, probably drunk, singing or swearing or throwing rocks through the windows of nearby stores. Some are carrying naked swords with them. They are loud and nasty. They are the "rakes," gangs of young men who flaunt their money and raise hell. They're bored, vicious, and insulting. They're on their way to the theatre but they would prefer to be the show rather than the performers.

We turn the block and spot Covent Garden Theatre. This afternoon they are advertising a play called *Love in aTub,* written by George Etherege. Lots of people are lining up to see the show but not us. We find a couple of thugs hanging around and pay them some pennies to stand in line. It was dangerous to stand in line since there were thieves around who might press in behind us, slit our kidneys, and then steal our places. The thugs will stand in line and just as they get to the front we'll take their purses. Meanwhile we'll go across the street and drink a little gin mixed with hot cocoa (disgusting, right?). As we move into the theatre we are given a chit, or a token. We don't have to pay yet. After the first act of the show we can either stay or go. If we stay, we pay; if we go, we'll never find out how the shows ends unless we ask somebody. Or we can stay and try to avoid the chit taker who is also going to take our money. There are two places that we can sit in the theatre (three if we're women), one is the pit, aptly named. The pit is filled with tables where most of the rakes and those who want to raise a little hell will sit. Cards are provided so that the gentlemen and their girlfriends will be able to amuse themselves during the show. Then there is the balcony where we're going to sit. Long benches have been provided in the area hanging over the pit so that nicer folks can watch both the stage and the pit at the same time. On the sides of the theatre overlooking the pit a group of ladies sit. They are called vizzard ladies. They're whores. They wear masks over their faces in order to hide their identity. Of course, everybody knew who was behind the masks, so the whole thing was just a big la dolce vita game. Some rather famous ladies used to hang out with the vizzards causing tremendous scandals and many duels. The vizzard would yell at the rakes in the pit and make them offers, and the rakes would climb up the front of the vizzard boxes and have their way with the vizzards right there in the side boxes! During the time when everybody is sitting down on their benches or in their boxes or on their chairs, orange wenches would be running around selling fruit and candy. Some of us find ourselves kind of squeezed in. The benches hold about twenty but the owners of the theatre have oversold and they're trying to seat forty to a bench. Everybody gets to know everybody else very well. One of the patrons sitting at the end of the bench doesn't look too well. His eyes are staring straight ahead. His body smells worse than the average Restoration citizen. There is a green slime running out of his ears. There are dark circles around his blank eyes. The fleas seem to be hopping off his clothes rather frantically. We keep asking him to move down but he doesn't answer, but he doesn't resist when we all shove. Yes, you figured it out: he's dead. Don't bother to call the theatre manager; dead plague victims are all over the place. Nothing to worry about. They'll clean him up in a day or so.

There is an introductory act to which nobody pays any attention. A fellow actor, John Comelately, recites dirty poems which get a kind of a chuckle or two from a few of the people in the balcony. Suddenly a fight breaks out in the pit. One of the rakes was found to be cheating at cards. A near riot breaks out. Don't worry, they can't get up to the balcony. It is completely sealed off from the pit. The rakes calm down and then there is another before-play performance. A woman sings. She is very popular and a few people in the pit actually listen. Some throw coins and make sexy remarks to her. Some of the coins she picks up and slips down her bosom. Some she throws back to the rakes which causes everybody to laugh. If you listen hard you can hear the theatre manager locking the doors. The doors are locked in such a way that it requires several minutes to open them. In case of fire you wouldn't stand a chance. Fires can break out at any time because everything is lit with tallow candles, which also smell like something dying. At last the play is ready to begin. Out steps Lady Bracegirdle, one of the most popular actresses of the time. Yes, for the first time in Western history we have a legitimate (well, almost) actress. Women are finally allowed to pursue a career on the stage. As she steps out, a few of the rakes and even some gentlemen of note and social position come out with her. They've been with her in the back of the theatre in a place called a greenroom. All the actresses serviced the audience when they could. Some of the men pull up chairs on the stage and sit and watch the ample Lady Bracegirdle do her stuff. As the play continues, it is obvious that the rakes are bored with it. Some of them throw garbage up on the stage at some of the less popular actors. Some of the rakes begin singing songs trying to drown them out. At the end of the first act very few people leave even through the show isn't very good, because it looks as if the rakes are going to provide a pretty interesting show themselves. The chit takers swarm all over the theatre, collect a few pennies here and a few pennies there. Some of the patrons try to hide under the benches or inside the vizzard boxes but they are discovered, and sometimes the more brutal chit takers make the attempted thieves pay double. At last the show begins again after a few introductory songs and poems. After the money was collected the quality of the show dropped off dramatically. The Restoration playwrights knew that all they had to do was keep their audience in the theatre for only one act and they had done their job. So, the first acts of most Restoration plays were really exciting but after that there was a definite lack of care. *Love in a Tub* was no exception. The one saving grace of the play was Lady Bracegirdle. The lady was definitely an asset to the production. First, she was voluptuous in the true Restoration style. Secondly, she was actually a pretty good actress. If you were in the theatre watching her, it would not be uncommon to see many men, and some of the women, appreciating her "work." Yes, that's right. That was one of the reasons the theatre was so popular. Somewhere during the fourth act of the play, a major fight breaks out in the theatre. No doubt one of the rakes who has been drinking gin for three hours had finally gone mad and started a riot. People up in the balcony with us love it. The rakes are beating each other to pulp, vizzards are being thrown out of the boxes, and the actors have finally given up and gone home. The management opens the doors to the theatre and we all start to leave. We mention the body to somebody at the door but he doesn't seem to understand.

Once out in the night air, everything seems very different. We had gotten used to the smell of tallow wax and the roar of noise all during the show. Somehow the air smells wonderful and the fading voices of the theatre patrons gives us a rather lonely feeling. We head back to our lodging across St. James park and we hear something that turns our blood to ice water. We hear a scream, a child's scream. It isn't the scream of a child who is just being spanked, or even just tortured. It was the cry of a dying child, a murdered child. It was a death scream in a jungle, for that is what London has turned into now. We quicken our steps but there ahead of us is a group of rakes trying to throw somebody into the lake. They spot us; they start to come after us. We run. It's dark in St. James and we're not exactly sure of where we're going. We can hear the yells getting closer. If they catch us after this long run, there will be the devil to pay. We hear a gun shot. One of the fools has a pistol and he's firing at us! We come around a corner and run into a blind alley. There's a wall in front of us. We turn around and the pack has caught up to us. It's all over. They'll probably kill us. They draw their swords and advance on us. And then they stop. Why? The wall that we had run into was St. James Palace. And there is the King's Coach coming down the stone path with a troop of soldiers escorting the coach. The rakes slink back into the darkness. They'll face most anything in London except the king. We bow as the coach goes by but we quickly follow it for a few blocks until we arrive safely at home. We step over a few drunks and close the door behind us, locking it several times.

If it sounds like it's more of a zoo than a city, you're not too far off. It was a wild time and the theatre met the needs of the people. Just as our theatre tries to capture the needs of the public, Restoration theatre reflected the lives of the citizens. They wanted to see themselves on the stage. They wanted the gossip of the city brought to life with real live actors. If you look closely at such shows at *Dallas, Falcon's Crest,* you are seeing pretty good examples of Restoration Theatre. You are seeing the lives of people who are not worth much to society. Yet their lives are presented in the most exciting and sexual way possible. Unfortunately, most of the Restoration plays you see today are cleaned up so much that they have lost whatever charm that they had in the first place, but if they were presented as they were performed three hundred years ago, then you would enjoy them as much as any of the so-called adult soap operas.

There is something else, one last idea that is important to us. During the Restoration period there was a very strong feeling that religion was no longer really important since the goal of life was life itself. The heavy ingestion of drugs, the lack of concern for morality, the heavy drinking all took its toll on the human personality. The same thing is happening now. And it isn't all just due to the ingestion of drugs and drink that has destroyed our human personality. It is more complex than that. There is an anger here in our society that manifests itself in our movies. Sure we have our share of *E.T.*'s, thank God, but we also have our share of Hell Raisers. In both societies the anger that was felt by the lonely and somewhat overdrugged Restoration society is the same anger felt in our lonely and very much overdrugged society. *The Rocky Horror Picture Show* is the perfect example of the kind of entertainment that fits into the category of the Restoration gone mad. Antisociety, anti-art, anti-love. You know a society is really crazed when it would rather watch lust than love and to the Restoration citizens love was just a rather corny idea that was popular in decades past. So now the real issue is, do we feel the same? Do we like to watch movies about love or lust? At this time there is something of the lustlover in us with just enough of a spark of decency to still cry at wonderful theatrical experiences such as *E.T.* *E.T.* would never have had a chance in London of 1670 because the corrupt individual would have felt that the honest display of friendship and love was too silly and unreal for them. Have we gone that far? No. Will we go that far? It is possible. Very possible. What we must do now is draw upon those elements of theatre which also feed the element of drama. We must always remember, as the Restoration people forgot, that theatre is only a way of explaining drama. Just as *Speed* was merely an excuse to show chases and battles, the Restoration people needed theatre only as an excuse to enjoy sexual aberrations.

Charles II died of several diseases in 1685 and his brother James II became king. James II was a strong but dumb king and he lasted for three years. Parliament then invited William and Mary to become king and queen of England, and London began the slow process of cleaning itself up. William and Mary were religious people and soon put an end to the drugs, the abuse of gin, and the wild plays. Theatre became a little less interesting but far safer. By 1700 the Restoration period had come to an end much the way a bad case of food poisoning finally subsides. The city of London had been hanging its head over the bowl for a long time, nearly forty years, and now things were back to normal. One of the most interesting plays in the whole period came in 1700. *Way of the World,* written by William Congreve, took a look backwards and poked fun at the now harmless Restoration period. The play deals with an old lady named Lady Wishforit who has a young girl who is in love with a lad named Mirabel (I know it. Hard to tell the boy from the girl at this time). The old lady has so much cracked makeup on that her face looks like a spider web. The villain in the piece is a man named Fainall who is crafty and nasty. He wants to gyp the old lady out of her fortune, and she in turn doesn't want Milimont and Mirabel to marry because she thinks he is fortune hunter. The upshot of the play is that Fainall is punished (the villains were never punished in the old Restoration plays because the villains were the heroes) and Milimont and Mirabel get married. But before they do, Congreve gives them a scene which has to go down in history as the greatest women's rights essay before the ERA movement. Milimont is in love with Mirabel but she makes it very clear that she is not going to be one of those wives who has to put up with a husband who has several mistresses. In fact she tells him that he can't go to the theatre without her. And he can't drink hard stuff and in no way can he strike her. She demands fidelity and an equal partnership in all things. She also demands a private room of her own that he can't enter unless she gives him permission to do so. He accepts everything. However, he has a few demands to make himself. First, whenever she gets pregnant, she can't wear binding clothes so that his child will be suffocated in the womb. And she cannot go to the theatre and she will not be allowed to drink hard drinks. And most of all, she will not be allowed to entertain a man in her private room alone. She agrees to his terms and the pact is sealed. Nobody ever speaks a word about love. The marriage will develop into a love relationship, but for now it is a business union just as all marriages were in the Restoration period. And with *Way of the World* the last bit of Restoration period was laid to rest. Thank God.

There are so many strange things to learn from this perverted period of western theatre and drama that it would take several volumes to begin to discuss it. The fascination for drugs, sexual theatre of manners and the obsession to be part of the "king's" crowd has come down to us in all kinds of strange forms. First, the drug problem in this country was no less in severity than it was among "high" society in London in 1680. The only difference is that the English didn't know any laws against drug use. It brought their society into so much pain and agony that it was literally burned away with the great fire and plague of the Restoration period. The profusion of "lusty" theatre . . . nearly pornographic popular theatre comes down to us in the form of soap operas. Probably no other form of American entertainment has such a faithful audience as the soap addicts. If they miss an episode of *Lust For Life* or *All My Adulterers* they feel as if their lives are somehow incomplete. Restoration theatre is to blame for such trashy stuff. In fact you might even take all of those so-called talk shows which feature guests who have sexual stories to tell. You know what I mean. "Our topic today is, 'Transvestite Priests and their Sexual Fantasies'." A lot of Americans really eat up this kind of stuff. Yes, that's right. More Restoration influenced entertainment. But the most damaging result of the Restoration period was the blind pursuit of "fashion."

Charles II was such a magnetic character that everything he said, did, and wore influenced London in a big way. Charles set the fashion because he was the most powerful society personage in the country. Millions of dollars were spent in an attempt to keep pace with fashion. If the king felt that middle class values were useless then people began to replace middle class values with immorality! During the Restoration marriage became one of those mundane middle class values that suffered because Charles liked to make fun of marriage, fidelity, and family values. Charles had specific clothing ideas and "everybody who was anybody" copied his clothing sense. In *The Way of the World* it becomes so obvious how bad society *was* and good society *could be* in the next century. But here is the problem; we are still slaves to fashion. Sure you are! You see some popular geek on TV wearing his baseball cap backwards and suddenly that's a fashion statement. And if you want to be "cool" you'll wear your cap backwards too. Even if you hate the look you will still think it's cool to do it. If torn up jeans priced at $150 are popularly shown in magazines or on TV or in the movies you'll buy them and wear them. It's cool to be in fashion and being cool is really important! Why? You want people to think that you understand what the term "popular" means and being cool is one way to become popular. And being popular is never stupid . . . of course it is sometimes but you don't think so. So you've got to have Power Rangers, or ripped up shorts walk with beat up tennis shoes with no socks, or red stripes in you hair, or listen to some special music. But fashion demands that you do it . . . that you follow the lead set by fashion. And that is the legacy of the Restoration period in London which lasted from 1660 until 1700. So now you know that the "Restoration" means to restore to the throne. And it was Charles II who was restored but in a very real sense we are still suffering because of his reign!

CHAPTER SEVEN

Tear-out Study Guide

1. _____ was the king of England during the Restoration period.

2. The playwright Wycherly wrote a play called _____.

3. Another Restoration play was *Love in a* _____.

4. For the first time in Western history _____ are allowed to act on stage.

5. Restoration means to _____ to the throne.

6. The Restoration period in England lasted from _____to_____.

7. One of the characteristics of the Restoration period was an obsession with _____.

8. One of the elements of theatre that was the most prominent in Restoration theatre was _____.

9. In 1700 a play called _____ described marital relations during the Restoration period.

10. During the Restoration period the art of the _____ put down came into its own.

Passionate Romantics

This looks like the good chapter, right! Passionate sounds as if we're really going to get into theatre element number 2. Well, sorry, we won't . . . or at least not too much. Passionate Romanticism really has to do with an emotional state which makes it difficult for a person to contain his or her emotions. It has to do with all those passionate emotions that you have pent up inside of you and how you express them. Passionate Romantics (a Pa Ros) think with their emotions. Hormones dominate their lives; hormones which are going crazy! Passionate Romantics don't care what the consequences are when they do something! They just care about the actions! Today, we're experiencing the greatest crime wave in the history of our country and a great deal of that crime is drug related and gang related. Using drugs is a passionate romantic action. Belonging to a gang is a passionate romantic action. Passionate Romanticism was a movement that started centuries ago but we're just beginning to feel the negative impact of the movement as it manifests itself in movies, TV, and sports. A while ago a nationally ranked ice skater actually participated in a brutal attack on another nationally ranked ice skater. Passionate Romanticism at work again! A famous runner from Canada used drugs to become the fastest runner in the world. But drugs" Why drugs? Passionate Romanticism! When the 49ers won the fifth Super Bowl championship lots of people were screaming and vicariously playing that game with them, I certainly did. We were all Passionate Romantics.

I think when all is said and done Bill Clinton will go down in history as the Passionate Romantic president. And I'm not referring to all of those rumors about sexual infidelity. I'm talking about a president who always lets us know when his feelings get hurt! He always seems so disappointed and depressed when things don't go his way. Does he play poker? I hope not. He certainly wouldn't fool anybody and neither does the Passionate Romantic! Saddam Hussein and his "mother of all battles" line reveals himself to be a Passionate Romantic. To say that Pa Ros exaggerate, intensify, and make mountains out of mole hills is an understatement. *Married With Children* is a good example of Passionate Romanticism because nobody *thinks* in that TV series and everybody is totally selfish! Soap Operas are all good examples of Passionate Romanticism. *Natural Born Killers* is also a good example of Passionate Romanticism. Now, I can hear you saying, "I still don't get what this is all about . . . what's so bad about bragging and being committed to things? So I'll tell you. Balance. There is no balance in a Passionate Romantic. There is no message from that little voice in you that says, "Should you do this? Somebody could get hurt. Somebody could die. You could go to jail. Families will be ruined forever."

So how did all of this get started in the first place? When did this Passionate Romanticism thing get its birth? Well it came in a very unusual way and from a very unusual man. Our last chapter ended with the death of Charles II who would have been a good candidate for Passionate Romanticism's birth but he wasn't the one who started it.

We're not going to stay with Britain now in our search for our entertainment roots. Suffice to say in 1703 good Queen Anne became queen and life in England was rather nice. There was only one significant play produced during her reign call *Cato*, by Joseph Addison, but today we would simply find it the most boring of plays. For our purposes we are going to move to Germany (there was no real Germany until 1870 but this is close enough). We are about to explore one of the most fascinating and interesting aspects of entertainment. There is no question in my mind that what we are about to explore is going to knock you out because all of you have experienced Passionate Romanticism, but few of you have taken the time to realize how entertaining it can be. Most of the time we are suffering as Passionate Romantics rather than enjoying the experience. First let's review a bit. From the ancient Greeks to the present time, 1775, Theatre and Drama had developed into an excellent means of entertainment. Under Shakespeare it hit its highest level. But nobody had really tried to understand the real nature of entertainment until the late Eighteenth Century. What I mean by that is we keep asking the question "why". Why is this entertaining? Why is Jonsonizing interesting to experience? Why does the pornography of Restoration period seem so interesting? Why does the Roman sense of violence really transcend the centuries and make it to modern movies? Why do we as Americans feel as much for love as for violence? Why do we have such a catholicity of taste? Why do we really want to be entertained? All of these questions can be answered through a real examination of Passionate Romantic movement which we still have not finished as you sit here reading this text.

First let us understand what Passionate Romanticism means. Don't confuse it with the hot and ready passion of a drive-in movie experience, although it is possible that it could be part of the definition. It doesn't have anything to do with necking in your living room although it is possible that part of that experience could also involve necking. The Passionate Romantic is the naked *id* coming to the surface of our consciousness and dominating our actions; in other words, we act crazy.

In 1775 a German writer named Johann Goethe (pronounced Gerta) published a book called *(Sorrows of Young Werther*. The book turned our lives upside-down. The book spread through Europe like wildfire. The book basically dealt with a boy named Werther whose life was so miserable, so sad that sadness becomes an enjoyable thing. Werther loved but he was not loved back. He tried to succeed and failed. He tried to develop pride and it resulted in loss of pride. Everything he did met with failure, and through this loss of everything that he had thought was brilliant in his life, he Werther, found dark. And what is more important he let everybody know how sad and miserable he was. He kept nothing to himself. His need to suffer became so apparent that people began to understand that he was a very unique person. They didn't like him or respect him; they began to notice him. The more he was noticed for doing strange and sad things, the more he continued to do them. Soon he became a hero in his own mind for failing at everything. He was a sad pitiful little person whose sadness reached into our own lives and completely made us happy! Weird? Yeah, it was, but it was also interesting. Goethe then wrote a play called *Faust*. Those of you who have more than just a mediocre high school education know that in the Elizabethan period a playwright named Marlowe also wrote a play based on the legend of Faust. Basically, Goethe took the same legend but turned it into a real example of Passionate Romanticism. Goethe's *Faust* deals with a scientist who is trying to unlock the door to ultimate power and in the process he summons up an "angel" from hell. The devil's representative tells Faust that the devil has consented to give him anything he wishes. Faust realizes that he has ultimate power so he begins to wish for everything. But it doesn't work out; he trades his soul to the devil just so he can have power and no matter what he wants it seems unsatisfying. In the end the devil comes to collect Faust, who does not want to go to hell after the devil has tricked him out of all the pleasures of the real world. Here is one play that I will not give away because I think it is really important that you read it yourself. You'll find it very exciting and pretty erotic. Give it a shot after we finish our discussion of Passionate Romanticism. The end of the play is exciting and maybe not what you expected.

After *Sorrow of Young Werther* and *Faust*, Goethe was the recognized leader of a new movement but nobody knew what to call it. It was easy to describe: First, people seemed to let their emotions go. If you feel it, you do it. Two, there seemed to be a real love of nature and especially storms and rain. Three, there was a real sense of suicide in the person who is a Passionate Romantic. Four, the Passionate Romantic is selfish. Five, the Passionate Romantic is very fickle. Six, the Passionate Romantic falls in and out of love very fast. The Passionate Romantic is dedicated to causes but not to logic. Seven, the Passionate romantic thinks with his emotions, not his brain. Eight, the Passionate Romantic is a real loner. All of these descriptions came out of the work done by Goethe and his friend and co-worker Schiller. By 1800 the Passionate Romantic movement was in such full swing that people outside of Europe, in Africa and in China, were getting copies of *Sorrows of Young Werther* and they were getting into Passionate Romanticism.

For centuries the true nature of people had never been allowed to be expressed but now with Werther letting it all hang out, people began letting their natures hang out too. People began writing love poems to each other. People who could not explain sadness in any other way complained of "soul sadness," a typical complaint of the Passionate Romantic. The suicide rate went up drastically in Europe and especially in the German states. The entire nature of the human spirit was exposed to a new emotional virus and anybody who came into contact with it seemed to succumb to its exciting symptoms. The point of all this is, we are all infected sometime during our lives. And I believe that this Passionate Romantic tendency in us tends to make us appreciate a certain kind of entertainment which is definitely another aspect of our definition of Theatre.

I think the best definition of the true Passionate Romantic and all of the characteristics of the Pa. Ro. is one which you might find very familiar because one thing that all Pa. Ros have in common is love. All of us have bad love affairs and the Pa. Ro. tends to have more of them than the average person. The story was told to me by a student a few years ago who had missed about three weeks of one of my drama classes. Then one day she just happened to come into my office crying like a baby. She was really upset; so I told her to sit down and tell me about it, but she said she was too upset to talk so she started to walk out of the door. Then she turned around and came back crying again. I told her that she could talk about it if she wanted to but no, she didn't want to. This is a lie. All Pa. Ros want to talk about their problems. She headed for the door again and actually went through it but in a second she was back. She sat down in a chair and started the tale of pain. It seems that six months ago she had been dating a lot of boys, just playing the field and then just like a lightning strike she met Victor. Victor was a big man on campus. He had lettered in twenty-five sports, was an All-American, All-European, and All-Ego. Every woman on campus drooled every time Victor waved his B.O. ridden sweatshirt. She met Victor at a sorority-fraternity dance and it was love at first sight (it had happened to Victor the first time he looked into a mirror). All of her sorority sisters thought she was the luckiest girl in the world. I mean, gee, who would want anybody better than Victor. The cute way he would look at her and whisper in her ear, "Ughgh." When he was hungry he would gently say, "food." And when he felt romantic he would so sweetly say, "Bed." Yes, he was every woman's dream. Of course there were certain things about Victor that she didn't like, such as the way he walked with his arm around her waist fondling her breasts with his fingers. It was a little embarrassing, but when in love these kinds of things don't mean much. And, of course, there were those moments of compensation when Victor would be about to slam a ball through the water polo goal and then point his finger up in the stands where she was waiting and he would seem to say, "This one is for you, baby." She would faint. All of her sorority sisters were so jealous. She loved it. Then after a month he told her that it would be better for the relationship if she moved out of the sorority house and into an apartment so that they could be more alone. Of course, he didn't say it exactly that way. What he had said was, "More food. More bed." And, of course, she interpreted it that he wanted a stronger relationship. When you're in love you don't have to hear it all to know what is meant. So she moved into an apartment across from school. Then every night Victor would come to her house, let her make dinner for him, let him do with her whatever he wanted. She did things that she knew that only "bad" girls do but, because she loved Victor, she did them anyway because she loved him. She had called her mother in Sacramento and told her how much she loved

Victor, and she told her that she wanted to plan a June wedding. She had already picked out her pattern and was just waiting for the moment when Victor would pop the question or even say that he loved her. She was waiting for Victor to come over one evening, just waiting and visualizing what their children would look like. She did that a great deal now. Now that she was going to get married, she didn't really take an active interest in school because she wouldn't need it to do what she really wanted to do with her life. Of course, she had to help Victor, so she had enrolled in a great many courses in the Ag. Dept., even though she was an art major. But it didn't make any difference. Victor had needed the help and she was glad to give it. So it was on such a night when all these things were going through her head that the phone ran. She answered it. It was Victor. She recognized his grunt. "When are you coming over, sweetheart?" she cooed. There was silence on the phone and then Victor spoke. "Forget it. It's all over. Hate you. Never want to see you again. Drop dead." He hung up. She couldn't believe it. It must have been one of Victor's friends having a little fun with her. She dialed back. Victor's phone rang. A woman answered it. "Is Victor there, please." The woman told her to hang on. Victor had just grabbed a beer. She could hear laughing in the background. Then Victor answered. She began to get nervous. "Victor, did you just call me?" "Yeah. Drop dead." Victor, what are you doing? Is this some kind of a joke? I mean all the things that we are to each other..." He cut her off and hung up. She sat there crying on the phone. She hung up. "I'm not going to call him. If he wants to talk with me, he'll have to call me. That's all there is to it. I'm humiliated. I'm scared. I'm angry. I'm going to call." Quickly her fingers hit the buttons. The phone rang and rang. Finally the woman picked up. "I want to talk to Victor." "He's got his pants off and he can't come to the phone." There was laughing in the background and she hung up the phone. Completely humiliated, she desperately wants to talk to Victor. She thinks that by talking to Victor that she will be able to change his mind about his decision to dump her. The Passionate Romantic always thinks that because his or her feeling is so deep that given the time and opportunity, he or she can change the mind of someone who doesn't want to associate with them in a romantic way. The Pa. Ro. is positive that the reason the person doesn't want him or her is a mistake. She punches the buttons, it rings. This time Victor answers. "Go to hell." Hangs up. She puts the phone down. Her tummy starts to wretch. Her whole life has just gone down the drain. She begins to cry. Long loud sobs. She wants to die. She is going through agony. Over what? Over a 40 IQ twit who isn't good enough to hold her shoe, let alone marry her. But she doesn't care about that. She is in love. She can't use logic here; she can only think about her entire life washed up. Twenty-two years old and she has nothing to live for. She wants to die. She runs to the medicine cabinet and looks in. Nothing but bandaids and listerine. Nuts! She runs back to the phone. No, she won't call. She's got to get her mind off the phone. She turns on the radio . . . big mistake. For Passionate Romantics there are always messages in the music that comes over the radio waves. "Breaking Up is Hard To

Do" screams the lyrics to a rock song. She races over and turns the dial. "You Said You Loved Me But You Didn't Mean It." She turns the dial again. "I Can't Live Without You." She turns off the radio and throws herself on the couch. The Passionate Romantic always thinks that a bad break is something personal. God must hate her. Why else would He punish her? She screams. "God, please give me back Victor and I'll do anything, anything. I promise I won't ever smoke a joint again!" Bargaining is also part of being a Pa. Ro. Suddenly the phone rings. "Thank You, God," she screams as she races to the phone, her heart beating, her palms sweaty, her makeup running all over her face. "Hello, Victor." The voice on the other end is not Victor's. It is Herbie's. Who is Herbie? There is always a Herbie in the life of a Pa. Ro. Herbie is the little pest who is always trying to follow you around. In the case of Herbie it was love and hate at first sight. Herbie loved her and she hated Herbie. She always wondered why Herbie wouldn't take no for an answer. From the first time in class when she saw him drooling on his geography book, she thought he was a nerd. The first day he came up to her and introduced himself. "Hi, my name is Herbie Manilare. I'm a Freshman. Can I walk with you?" Looking at Herbie's face reminded her of the time when she used to make topographical maps in the sixth grade. Herbie and puberty had been having a tough time. She noticed that he had eaten soft boiled eggs for breakfast because some of the yolk had dried and stuck in the corners of his mouth. He wore tight jeans. He must have been expecting a flood. If the cuffs were any higher, they could have been gym shorts. He wore a sweater with a high school letter on it. He had been assistant manager of the table tennis team. He wore black and white tennis shoes with his name written on sides where the rubber meets the canvas. Herbie was on the phone, not Victor. How did he get her number? Very simple. He noticed her car one day and called Vehicle Registration at the State Capitol, claimed he was an insurance agent and needed her address and phone number so he could settle a claim. You see, Herbie is a Passionate Romantic too. "Hi," said Herbie. "Can't talk now, Herbie," she says with tears in her voice. "What's wrong, what's wrong, what's wrong? Can I help? Please! Please! Please! Let me help! Oh, I want to help! Please! Please! Please!" Herbie is dying to be a friend. And she really wants to talk to somebody about all of this, but who? Her mother? No way. Her sorority sisters? Too humiliating. Herbie is the only one she can talk to. All she wants to do as a Pa. Ro. is talk and the more unimportant the person is the better. O.K., she'll take a chance and talk to him. She has got to talk to somebody or she's going to commit a Listerine overdose. "Herbie, listen, I do want to talk to somebody about a problem." Herbie screams, "I'll be right over, we'll get something to eat, I know this really neat place, I'll be right over." And before she can say no, she just wants to talk on the phone, Herbie hangs up. She really doesn't want to see him but then again, if she talks to him on the phone, then the line will be busy, and if Victor is trying to call her, he won't get through. Right now she would give anything in the world if he would just call back without any problem. Pa. Ros keep up this foolish hope that human nature will change.

In exactly twelve minutes Herbie covers the distance between her apartment and his parents' house (a distance of some twenty-five miles). And he has had time to shave and buy a new set of "threads." When she opens the door the worst Herbie image she has ever seen is standing there. In his attempt to hurry, Herbie has cut his topographical face many times. He has left some of the toilet paper bandaids on his throat. Little red dots are still forming. Also he didn't bother to get all of the shaving cream out of his sideburns and it has dried there. It tends to flake off every time he speaks. He bought a new Levi coat on the way over and they obviously didn't have his size. The sleeves are rolled up at the cuffs. "Hi," he says. He walks in. "Now look, Herbie, I don't want anything to eat, I just want to talk." Herbie's face drops and looks as if he's about to cry. "Really, we don't have to do anything big, and I didn't eat anything yet, and if you're really upset, it will do you good to get out, really. Come on, please, please!" He stands there bleeding and snow flaky about to cry. She does not want to be seen with him but then again she doesn't want to hurt his feelings, especially since he's going to spend the evening listening to her crying about Victor. And who knows, Herbie is smart; maybe he can suggest a way for her to get Victor back. She puts on her coat and takes the phone off the hook. If Victor tries to call, maybe he'll keep calling if he thinks she's at home. She goes downstairs with Herbie who keeps telling her how great she looks. His car is parked out in front. It's a 1964 Chrysler about 6" off the ground and painted pink, hand painted. Inside it appears to be one big fuzz ball. He opens the door and she sits, or rather sinks, on the front seat. For a moment she decides that she doesn't want to go out, but across the street she spots one of her sorority sisters and she ducks down instead. Herbie hops in and turns on the radio. There are speakers everywhere including under the seats. Of course, the music that she hears tells about lovers who don't get together, lovers who get together and then split, and lovers who don't want to be friends anymore. This is torture. Before Herbie drives to dinner he has to make a trip to his old high school. He drives around the parking lot and points with a big smile on his face. "Herbie, I want to talk but the music is too loud." He turns the music down. "I'm hungry, let's get something to eat. I know this really neat place, I go there all the time." He turns the car around and pulls up to Denny's. "O.K., let's get some food." She is really starting to get sick now. All she can think about is Victor and that woman who answers the phone. How could he do that? After all the things that she had done? "I'm going to have the fried chicken and the french fries and an order of french fried onion rings." She takes a cup of tea. "Now what is it that is bothering you?" At last she has a chance to talk. At last the Passionate Romantic can get it off her chest once and for all. (That's not true. The Passionate Romantic will repeat the same thing over and over until the pain begins to go away.) "Well, you know that Victor and I have been going. . . " All of a sudden the food comes and she stops talking a moment because the waitress is there and Herbie jumps in. "I'm majoring in auto mechanics. I want to fix cars for a living. See my wheels? I rebuilt the engine myself!" From then on Herbie talks about nothing but cars. She tries to break in but it is no good. Herbie is on a roll! And what is worse, nobody ever trained Herbie to be polite at the table. He talks and chews and spits all at the same time. The few times you glance his way are terrible. Plus, grease spots keep appearing on her blouse. She starts to get up. "Look Herbie, I wanted to talk about something, but all you've done is eat and tell me stories about spark plugs. I'm grabbing a cab and going home." Herbie jumps up and leaves money for his meal. "Gee, I'm sorry, come on please, give me a chance, please!" Everybody in the place is beginning to look. She goes through the door and tries to see a cab. Herbie follows. "Look, how about getting a drink?" For the first time tonight Herbie has said something that makes sense. "A drink," she says. "I need a drink, Herbie." They jump in the car. "I know a place that my uncle took me to once." What she would like is a nice quiet little bar where she can get several creamy drinks and forget Victor for just a minute or two. Twenty minutes later Herbie pulls up to a joint on the wrong side of town. "Herbie, I don't think I want to go in here." "It's O.K., I know the place. It's great. Come on." She gets out of the car and walks through the doors with Herbie leading the way. The place is nearly empty. An old man is standing at the bar in a pool of some foul smelling liquid. There is a juke box in a corner playing "My Broken Heart." She wants to go but Herbie rushes to the bar and brings back two drinks, boilermakers. She takes one and sips it, and thinks about the time Victor and she were the stars of the Country Club Spring Dance just last week. She thought Victor was going to ask her to marry him that night but instead he simply lifted her skirts and had intercourse with her behind the wedding chapel on the eighteenth green and then he got sick.

Three hours later and six trips to the bathroom at the Chevron station across the street and she is ready to go home. So is Herbie. Thirty minutes later she's trying to climb out of his car and he's helping her. "No, Herbie, I can get in upstairs, O.K." "No, let me help you, besides we haven't talked yet, and I'm really thirsty. All that drinking made me really thirsty. Could I come in?" She feels a little dizzy, so she says that it would be O.K. for Herbie to come in and get a glass of water and then go. The moment she enters the apartment she puts the phone back on the hook. Meanwhile, Herbie has found some wine and he's offering her a glass. "Herbie, I don't want any wine, and it's late and I'm expecting an important call." "Please, just one glass. One glass and I'll go." She settles back into the couch, hardly noticing that Herbie has sat down beside her. She takes a glass of wine and then falls asleep. She wakes up in the morning and looks out of the window. It is raining. She thinks of Victor and somehow the rain makes her feel a little better. She notices that the clock say 11:45 a.m. She and Victor have had a standing date for six months at the student union every afternoon. She throws back the cover to get out of bed and suddenly notices a lump. She feels a little dizzy and can't quite remember what the lump was in the bed. All of a sudden the lump moves. She throws back the covers and there is Herbie. He is lying there with pants pushed down to his ankles, his mouth wide open. A wave of nausea sweeps over her as she rushes to the bathroom. In the middle of the night Herbie had to rush to the bathroom too . . . he missed the toilet. She jumps into the shower. Her body has been violated by the worst of all possible violations: Herbie. No matter how much water and soap she uses, she can't seem to get the smell of french fried chicken off her body. It's in her pores! She comes rushing out of the shower. She throws a pair of jeans on and a top just as Herbie starts to awaken. He spots her. "I love you," he says. She almost passes out. "Get out of here," she screams. Herbie looks puzzled. "But last night you said you loved me." "Get out of here." She drags him from the bed and throws him out in the hall. "I'll get my things and move in tonight." Herbie runs down the stairs. Her head is pounding. It's raining heavily now and she is not wearing any coat. She runs across the campus dashes into the student union. There sitting in their usual spot is Victor, and so is a dark haired girl with big breasts. She stands across the room from Victor, dripping wet. A couple of her sorority sisters come up to her and try to offer condolences. She starts to cry. She decides to go straight up to Victor and have it out with him. Victor looks up and grunts. This is the moment of truth for all Passionate Romantics: she is facing the man she loves without understanding why he doesn't love her and why he won't talk to her. She is sure that if he will only talk to her, then she will get him back. She's nervous. She knows everybody is looking at her. Victor doesn't say a word. "Could I speak with you Victor?" She starts to cry again. Victor looks uncomfortable but he doesn't say anything. "Please I would like to talk. I won't keep you long." Victor finally grunts something about being too busy. Her entire life is crumbling, her heart is breaking, she wants to die and he doesn't even have the humanity to say *I'm sorry.* (The Passionate Romantic always assumes that everybody ought to have humanity but wouldn't she act the same way if she were the one dropping Victor?) She turns and runs out of the union. As she is climbing up the stairs in the rain she spots Herbie who is waiting for her. He says, "I love you." She looks at him as if he is a slug. "I hate you, you slimy idiot. I never want to see you again!" (Well now we know how much humanity she has.) Herbie stands there shocked. Then he turns and walks away. He is crushed. As he is walking a skinny little girl follows him and asking if he would like to talk about it. She watches them go. She looks back at the union and then begins to cry as she walks back to her apartment.

O.K., get the picture? Sound familiar? How many of you have gone through the agony or are going through that agony right now? You think that you'll never survive the experience but you do. It is all part of being a Passionate Romantic. Now how does this all hook up to entertainment? Well if you haven't guessed, Passionate Romanticism has been in the movies and on stage for fifty years. When you sit in that dark room and look up at the screen and all of a sudden you feel sad or happy or angry or exhilarated, then you are participating in Passionate Romantic experience. We go through it every time we come face to face with any kind of a crisis. The younger we are, the more crisis points. Let me give you a few more examples. The other day I was in a grocery store pushing around my cart when all of a sudden I saw this little kid reach up, grab some marshmallows and throw them in the basket. His mother said that he couldn't have them and that he had to put them back on the shelf. The kid said, "no." Just like that, "No." The mother reached into the basket and put the marshmallows back. the kid began to scream and yell that he wasn't loved and that he was hated and that he would die if he didn't get any of those marshmallows. The mother told him to be quiet but the kid refused to stop crying. The kid screamed, "Everything always happens to me, everything always happens!" The mother reasoned with the child, pleaded with the child and finally threatened the child. Nothing worked. At last the mother put the marshmallows back in the basket. The kid won. The little Passionate Romantic won. He screamed and threw his emotional weight around until the mother could not stand the pressure. The kid Romanized her, Jonsonized her, and Passionate Romanticized her all in two minutes and twenty-eight seconds. Now this is natural. To kids, problems are always life and death. When the problems are life and death and don't amount to a hill of beans, then you know that you've got a serious Pa. Ro. problem. For example, how many people do you know read the paper and come away screaming at things that they can't change? How many people hear about a cause of some kind and immediately become a super supporter of it without really knowing what it is all about? Back in the Viet Nam days the whole hippie reaction to life was an example of Passionate Romanticism. And today the punk movement is another Pa. Ro. reaction. Anything that makes the person respond with his emotions rather than his brain fits into the Pa. Ro. movement. How many of you go to *Rocky III* or I or II and yell or applaud out loud in the movie? Lots of you do, but can the actors hear? No, of course not, but the Passionate Romantic doesn't care if anybody hears it as long as he does it.

If you can remember James Dean, then you know that he was the hottest of all the Passionate Romantics. He was a rebel who fascinated women by showing them his pain and his cool. Grace under pressure was Dean's style. Brando was the same. Sometimes they could be little boys throwing fits and then they could be worldly men throwing passes at beautiful women. James Bond's 007 is a Passionate Romantic, a man who risks his life for his ideals, his country, and his sex life. *Chariots of Fire* is the best example of Passionate Romantic film made in 1982. For those of you who don't know the film it is one that has all of the elements that make up the positive side of the Passionate Romantic nature. The film takes place in the early 1920's in England. A Jewish man has just entered Cambridge and it is his goal to become the greatest track star in the world. Meanwhile, a Christian man in Scotland wants to become the greatest tract star in the world in the name of Christ. Both stories develop the ego, the courage, and the resolve of both men until we find them at the 1924 Olympics in Paris. The   Christian learns that his race falls on a Sunday and he was sworn not to run on the Sabbath. When the British Olympic Committee hears about this, they blow up. They even bring in the Prince of Wales, the future King of England, to try to persuade him to run, but it does no good. He sticks to his resolve. He is a true Pa. Ro. in that once he decides something is right, then nothing, no logic, no force, nothing can change his mind. Meanwhile, the Jewish runner has barely made it to the finals of the dash. He has come in second each time, but now he has to summon up every ounce of courage and strength to win his race. The gun goes off, the racers leap to the contest, and the Jewish runner throws every strength of will into the race and wins! The audience goes crazy as the film runs the race over and over. Then an interesting thing happens; one of the racers who was supposed to have run a distance race decides to let the Christian runner run in his place. Everybody agrees and the Pa. Ro. takes his place in a race where he is not supposed to do well at all. The coach of the other team (the Americans) feel confident that the Christian doesn't have a chance. The gun goes off and the race is on. The Christian summons up every ounce of courage and will and wins. The crowd goes crazy and the film shows us the race again. All of this is designed to make the hair go up on the back of your neck and explore what sense of Passionate Romanticism is in you. If you are a person who roots for the underdog, then you loved this movie and also love Passionate Romanticism. If you're the kind of person who doesn't particularly care for glory, then you are immune to the effects of Pa. Ro..

If you saw the film *Star Wars,* then you say the perfect blending of Passionate Romanticism and Bravado. These elements normally go hand in hand anyway. Hans Solo is the great Passionate Romantic who tries not to be one. He tries to be practical but he can't be. Only a Passionate Romantic would go against the odds to help a friend. The Passionate Romantic will also get you killed as he leads the soldiers into battle when he can't possible win. Most lunatics are Passionate Romantics because they see the world through such a narrow view. *Star Wars* is filled with such lunatics. Most of them are the villains but there is no doubt that Obi One Knobi is a Pa. Ro. He believes and practices the "force." He tells Luke to let go and let his intuition take over, and that is exactly what a Pa. Ro. would do. Most of us really like that idea of intuition guiding us over skill and logic. When we watch somebody who uses that kind of "go for it" attitude, we applaud because the Pa. Ro. force in us has been released and we immediately identify with such a person.

And as long as we're talking about intuition, then we should also talk about gambling. The Passionate Romantic always says I'm going to break the bank. The Passionate Romantic always thinks that "luck" will turn. Make an experiment for yourself. Take a trip to Reno or Las Vegas and observe the gambling Pa. Ro. in his native jungle. Watch the little old lady from Pasadena sit there with five hundred dimes in a paper cup. Watch her eyes light up when she hits a little jackpot. Does she take her dimes and run? Does she count up to see if she is ahead? Of course not, this little old lady who screams about overspending when she reads her newspaper is glued to the machine. She is typical of the Pa. Ro.. A few years ago James Caan made a movie called *The Gambler*. The movie claimed that gambling is a disease, a sickness that causes you to test your luck against the establishment because the thrill of winning is bigger than any thrill that exists in the universe. That thrill is also the rush the Pa. Ro. gets when he or she allows emotions to dominate logic. One day in Caesar's Palace I watched a gentleman foreign to this country drop $100,000 at the dice tables in about five minutes. He turned right around and got another $100,000 and promptly won back the money that he had lost a few minutes before. But like the true Pa. Ro. he went upstairs (I couldn't resist following) and went to the heavyweight tables where he sat down to a $400,000 loss. The Pa. Ro. was furious. He cursed some unknown god and then cursed luck (we all know her) and then asked for more credit. The management denied him the credit. He became furious and demanded more money. Eventually he got it. His luck turned and he made more money back than he had lost. By now a crowd had gathered as the high roller began to "break the bank." He sat down to a high stakes poker match, just the gambler and the house. That's the way this Pa. Ro. wanted it. It was three a.m., the gambler had lost three hands in a row, not to mention two hundred thousand dollars. He pushed a pile of chips toward the pot. The management claimed that they could not accept the bet because there was a limit on such things. The house is never a Pa. Ro., but the gambler refused to accept this. He began making derisive comments about the guts of the house. At last, a gentleman wearing dark glasses and a silk bathrobe came to the table and approved the bet. One hand of showdown poker for five hundred thousand dollars. The hand began, the gambler turned an ace, the crowd behind him shouted. The gambler looked weak but confident. The house then turned an ace. Nobody cheered. A pair of aces for the gambler! The crowd went wild. A pair of aces for the house. Silence in the room. The next two cards, a six for the house and a three for the player. The last card. If the house drew a king, then the player lost. If the player drew the king, then the Pa. Ro. walked off with more money than anybody had ever won or lost at that table during an hour period. The player drew a king . . . the crowd mumbled to themselves. The house could lose unless it drew at least a king. The house drew a card. There was a moment of hesitation and then it flipped over. There was a scream from the crowd. . . a queen! The Pa. Ro. pulled in over $800,000 in chips. He had done it. He sat there stunned. Not happy. Not screaming. Just staring. The house, coldly and quietly, began to stack his chips. "What are you doing?" cried the Pa. Ro., "Let's keep playing." The dealer looked at the man in the bathrobe wearing the dark glasses. There was a nod. The cards were dealt for five card draw. By 10 a.m. the next morning the Pa. Ro. was broke.

Let us look at the greatest example of the Passionate Romantic in films today: Indiana Jones. He is bent on self destruction. Why else does indiana Jones risk his life every five minutes of the film? Why does he have a name like indiana? I mean people are called Harry or Mary, they are not called Indiana unless they are Pa. Ros and in that case the Pa. Ros want a name that will give them color and flare. Jones is a wonderful name but, if it is preceded by Sam, we are more likely to think of Mayberry R.F.D. than high adventure in the Amazon jungles. And then look at what Indiana does in the film. He starts out by losing an idol. Then he loses a girl. Then he loses an ark. The Pa. Ro. is a born loser, but you've got to love him every time you think that he is going to win. He is a high adventurer who loves adventure for adventure's sake. He likes action and so do you. He loves the thrill of the chase and so do you. He loves the sense of gamble and so do you. He loves the risk involved in matching wits with an enemy and so do you. He loves the thought that good can win out over evil and so do you (although there are Passionate Romantics who are evil, e.g. Hitler). He's not satisfied with anything and most of you think that you're that way too. He is impulsive, explosive, and action motivated, and most of you think that you're that way too. Everything that is passionate attracts him and it attracts you too. Everything that is noble, heroic, patriotic, and at the same time anti-establishment (work on that one!) and so are you. You are Indiana Jones! And when you're sitting there in the theatre with your teeth clenched and your hands gripped around the handles of the chair watching Indiana climb up the front of a moving truck with a bullet in his arm, you're actually feeling the pain! Why? Because the Passionate Romantic nature in you is dying to come out and take over, and your ego keeps suppressing it but when a crazed person like Indiana Jones comes on the screen, much bigger than life, more healthy than all of us, more virile than the most virile of us, your Pa. Ro. nature is released through the concentration that it takes to follow the plot and the story. Once the door to your nature is unlocked, then you are lost to Passionate Romanticism. I mean there are some of us who have never fought a cobra, strangely enough, and the chance to fight one through the passionate nature of Indiana Jones is just too tempting to pass up. Now, realistically, there are some of you who are right now saying, "Big deal, who cares about dumb Indiana Jones?" You are not a Pa. Ro. or your Pa. Ro. nature is so buried that it is going to take more than an African adventurer to bring it out. Perhaps Greta Garbo could bring it out? Perhaps Charles Boyer lighting a cigarette, seductively looking at you as he slips the diamond ring he has just brought you on your finger, could bring it out of you? Somewhere the Pa. Ro. is in you and waiting to come out. This is the strongest artistic force in you. *It is there.* We have not evolved enough to loose it. Even the stonefaced Mr. Spock (Star Trek, not babies) has Pa. Ro. in him waiting to come out. Passionate Romanticism is part of the complete animal nature which we were born to use. When the first time a man-like thing stepped out of the primordial ooze of the African jungle and admired the ferocity of the other creatures, our Passionate Romantic natures were released. When David of Psalms cried out in the wilderness for help, he used his Passionate Romantic nature. When Jesus chased the money lenders out of the temple, it was a demonstration of his Passionate Romantic nature. When on the cross he cried "My God, My God, why have You forsaken Me?" it was a pouring forth of the Passionate Romantic. When you see John Wayne come riding down the street exercising all the *Bravado* in the world firing his guns and cursing the devil that made him, he is a Passionate Romantic. The popularity of Bert Reynolds is a tribute to Passionate Romanticism. He is the wild and crazy superstar who seduces women, races cars, blows up bridges, smuggles moonshine under the cop's nose and makes every other man in the world seem inferior because of his supreme confidence. He is the American answer to every European who thought he was the last word in suave . . . only Bert pronounces it sworve.

The problem with being a Passionate Romantic is that it is not just nice people who are Passionate Romantics. Hitler was a Passionate Romantic. His government did not last for a thousand years even though he bragged that it would. A Passionate Romantic makes exaggerated comments, takes theory and convinces people that it is fact, and can make the truth a lie and a lie the truth. Napoleon was a Passionate Romantic and so was General George Patton and Colonel Custer. When a Passionate Romantic falls, he falls with a crash. Remember, the whole idea of Passionate Romanticism was based on the idea that people are basically children who never really grow up. If movies are designed for twelve year olds as most of us think they are, then no wonder that the Passionate Romantic movie is so popular.

As a natural reaction to the Passionate Romantic movement, there developed a movement called Classicism which was in direct opposition to Pa. Ro. movement. And interestingly enough it was championed by Wolfgang Goethe, the old leader of the Pa. Ro.. As Goethe got older he realized that self-control and restraint were more important than letting it all "hang out." And he switched leadership to the Classicists. Now who in blazes were the Classicists? They were those who said, "Now look, the brain is better than the groin so let us make decisions based on thought, reason, logic, restraint, reserve, and intelligence." The Classicists looked at Werther and said, "The kid is a loser, he's got nothing to offer us." They looked at Faust and said, "If Faust were as brainy as he was horny, then he would have realized that the devil never plays fair, that's why he's the devil." Now, everybody has a bit of the Classicist in them to go to war against the evil Passionate Romantic in them. You might want to think of it as the Passionate Romantic in you representing your id, while the Classicist represents your ego. The ego is always trying to restrain your id and your id is always trying to draw upon your reserves of raw courage, raw energy and raw pain. The Classicist looks at the world and says, "Let us look before we leap." The Pa. Ro. says, "Let's not look, let's just leap." The Classicist says, "Let's think things over before we go to war." The Passionate Romantic says, "War is glorious no matter what the consequences are." It was obvious to all except a great many of the Japanese that they could never win a war against the United States; nevertheless, they bombed Pearl Harbor, which led them down the road to destruction. The Japanese Passionate

Romantics sought glory and honor before anything else. The result was the A Bomb. The decision to use the A Bomb came out of thought and consideration. The decision to drop the A Bomb was a Classical one because the motivation was to save lives, end the war as soon as possible, and do it by making the enemy die, not the American soldiers. Even though it appeared as a dramatic and theatrical gesture, it was not. The Classicist says, "Look, if there are people starving in the world, that's too bad. It just leaves more food for the rest of us." The Pa. Ro. says, "How can we allow to see people starving in the world when so many of us are rich and could afford to save them?" The Pa. Ro. says, "The Constitution is the only law of the land and there are no guilty, only the mistaken." The Classicist will stand by and let thousands die if millions are saved. The P. Ro. will sacrifice himself needlessly to make a point about morality. The martyr is a Pa. Ro. while the man who says, "Did he have to die for what he believed?" is the Classicist. He who gives orders has a bit of the Pa. Ro. in him and he who asks questions in order to get facts has a bit of the Classicist in him. Green peace is a Passionate Romantic movement. The United States of America has been a Pa. Ro. during the Spanish American War and a Classicist during the Viet Nam War.

In the movies we have several examples of the Classicist. The first is *Dirty Harry*. We have a detective who creates a climate of assassination because he decides that the law is not doing its job. He hates the bleeding hearts who find no bad boys, just misunderstood boys. So he does society's job for it. The movie was a big box office hit because there is something in us that likes to see common sense (even if it is violent and terrifying) dominating emotions. Common sense in this movie is rational but tough on the moralists. While the Passionate Romantics claimed that *Dirty Harry* should be outlawed because it preached vigilantism, the average guy on the block kind of thought that Dirty Harry wasn't so bad as long as he was gunning down somebody else. After all, the papers are filled with the stories of gangsters, who get away with murder because the law is so concerned with civil rights that it forgets the rights of innocent citizens. One of the most startling beautiful movies of 1982 was a German one called *Das Boot*. It described what happened to German sailors in WWII. The film starts out as a Passionate Romantic film filled with glory and patriotism and ends with the harsh realities that war is rotten business. And the result is absolutely dynamic.

As we get older we get safer. As we get older we lose that wonderful sense of adventure that we had when we were kids. We lose our imagination and our freedom. As Passionate Romantic kids we will wait for hours to see a jet plane land at an airport. As Passionate Romantic kids we will get up at the break of dawn to get a picture of a fading moon or a special star. As Passionate Romantic kids we love to get a tan. As we get older our Classical nature tells us that tans look great but sometimes you get skin cancer from too much sun; I'd rather be pasty than scabby. As Classical oldies we would rather drive slowly on the straightaway than fast because it isn't worth the speeding ticket to get that rush from driving faster than the speed limit. As Classical types we are far more interested in pleasure than pain. A walk in the country can be refreshing but the Classic type will not walk so far as to hurt his feet. The Pa. Ro. will walk in nature's playground until his feet hurt, his eyes hurt, and he's covered in bird doo-doo. In a war the Classic general will add up the potential dead in a battle and, if the figure is not too high for the worth of the ground taken and there is a good risk that the battle will be successful, he will attack. The Pa. Ro. looks at the situation and says, "Damn the torpedoes, full speed ahead."

Let's take the classic example of both the Classical and the Passionate Romantic, the film *On The Waterfront*. If you haven't seen this film then you have missed one of the greatest dramatic events ever filmed. This is a film that appeals to all strata of society, to most age groups except the little ones, to most lovers of Passionate Romanticism and Classicism. The film was filmed in the early 1950's and it reveals some very important insights to American culture as well. O.K., here is the film and what we can learn from it. First, it takes place down on the docks in New York. The area is tough, jungle-like. The longshoremen work for a guy named Johnny Friendly who runs the union. The workers in a very Classical way have devised a system for getting along with the bosses of the union who both protect them and threaten them. If they want work they kick back part of their wages to the bosses. The cops have been trying to find somebody who will testify that these so-called elected officials are on the take. They find a guy named Joey who will testify. But the union finds the guy first and throws him off a building. A young ex-fighter named Terry sets up this guy, and, although he doesn't like the fact that the kid is killed, he is very Classical about the whole thing. If the guy was a fink then he ought to die. Terry reasons that the guy could have kept out of trouble if he just kept his nose clean and overlooked the scams on the docks. But there are some Passionate Romantics around who think that the murder was a crime against God and man. One of them is the priest who wants to find the murderer of Joey. Johnny Friendly tells Terry to keep an eye on the priest. Terry's brother is the second in command which is why Johnny Friendly keeps Terry around. Plus the fact Johnny Friendly kind of likes the kid because he's a pug now and Friendly made some dough off the kid when Terry was fighting. Terry keeps an eye on the priest and also runs into Joey's sister, Evie. From the moment Evie and Terry get together it is a clash of the Classical nature vs. The Passionate Romantic nature. Terry is the pure example of the Classicist. He weighs everything. What he wants doesn't exceed his needs. Evie, on the other hand, wants justice and truth which are real luxuries on the waterfront. She is idealistic, as all Pa. Ros are. She is idealistic and hopeful. Terry on the other hand is a pretty cold and tough kid, except when he plays with pigeons which he keeps on the roof of an apartment building. Slowly he begins to realize that maybe being a Classicist is not the way to happiness. Maybe he ought to testify before the crime commission on the activities of the union. Johnny Friendly begins to worry about Terry's loyalty and he orders Terry not to see Evie. In one of the greatest scenes ever filmed Terry and his brother (Marlon Brando played Terry and Rod Steiger played his brother, Charlie) have the typical conversation between Classicist and Passionate Romantic as Terry recalls what he could have been if he hadn't taken a dive. Terry says, "I could have been a contender." In that one soulful complaint Terry tells us that his hopes for glory and fame were dashed by a racketeer who wanted to make a great deal of money off the odds game by betting that Terry would not win the fight that would send one of the two fighters into a championship match. Terry lost it all on a rational and logical decision, although illegal, to throw the match. Charlie comes back with an offer that no classical individual could turn down. Charlie tells Terry that the union wants to give him a job on another dock where all he has to do is be a boss, collect graft, and do nothing. A perfect job. Terry looks at his brother and then makes up his mind that he can't trust him and leaves the taxi. A great deal is going through Terry's mind. He thinks of the day before when one of the longshoremen was killed when a box crushed him. He thinks about the speech the priest made over the body of the dead man as the union leaders were throwing garbage at him. He thinks of the passionate bravery of the priest who proclaims, "This is my church, boys," as hecklers try to tell him to go back where he came from. He remembers the priest taking a can right in the head but ignoring the blood as he urges the men to act like men. He remembers the look on Evie's face when she realized that nobody was going to bring to justice the murderer of her brother. Then he charges up to Evie's apartment and in a very unusual move he breaks down her door and kisses her. Well, he more than kisses her but I don't have time to feed your imaginations with any more right now. While these two are in a clinch, Terry hears his name begin called by the mobsters. He runs downstairs with Evie. A truck tries to run them down but Terry pulls them to safety. Then he spots his brother Charlie hanging on a wall. Johnny Friendly had him killed as a warning. The warning would have had an effect on a Classical person but Terry has now become a Passionate Romantic and the death of his brother makes him furious and reckless. The next day he shows up at the trial and for the first time in his life he does not act in a Classical manner. He takes his life in his hands and he finks on the mob. He spills his guts to the crime commission. At the end of his testimony Friendly threatens Terry. Again the threat would have had an effect on a Classical person but not on Terry. The next morning he goes down to the dock to look for work. The entire union hates him because he finked on one of their own even if it were on one of their own who had been a killer. Of course, there is no work for him because he is now an outsider. But Terry won't take this. He wants his rights. He challenges Johnny Friendly to come up and fight him. Friendly has been looking for this opportunity. He weighs about 220 pounds and Terry weighs about 160 pounds. The Classical person would think that the odds are very unfair, especially when Friendly has mobsters to back him up just in case Terry gets lucky. Terry doesn't even consider any of this. He wants blood, and he charges Friendly with all the fury of a wounded animal. The fight is ferocious. At last five guys are beating up Terry. They leave him, a bloody and battered loser. Meanwhile the union members see what is happening and their natural sense of the underdog comes to the surface. They want Terry to win, they want Terry to get up and show Friendly that he isn't beaten. They want Terry to get up and walk into the warehouse and defy Friendly. If Terry will get off the ground and walk to the head of the line he will make Passionate Romantics out of all the guys. Terry struggles to his feet; the music begins to build. The faces on the workers start to smile. They form a line behind Terry as he takes his place, ready to work. Johnny Friendly screams at the workers. He threatens them. He can't win. They aren't afraid of him. The classical gangster has succumbed to the modern Passionate Romantic hero.

The true Passionate Romantic is carried away by music while the true Classical type likes music, appreciates music, but doesn't lose his head over it. The true Passionate Romantic is an idealist, while the Classicist is a realist (sometimes it's just an excuse so you won't have to do something that requires a commitment). The Passionate Romantic is described as a liberal democrat while a Classicist is a conservative republican. A Passionate Romantic is a person who does not have money, yet he likes to spend it. A Classicist has money, only spends it on things that will get him more money. A Passionate Romantic is a spouse who makes mad passionate love to you one night and can't remember your name the next. The Classicist will marry for stability, wealth, and compatibility. You may not have an exciting time with a Classicist, but you won't have to wonder if he is coming home at night. Passionate Romantics are fun people but you can't always rely on them or trust them. A Classicist may be a crook but he doesn't try to cover up his crookedness by claiming that his actions were for the "good of the people." A crazed person who hijacks a plane in order to bring light on a subject is a Pa. Ro., but a person who hijacks a plane because he thinks he can get away with it and earn himself a big reward at the same time is a Classicist. The Passionate Romantic crams for a test, while the Classicist studies every day until the job is done. True, the Pa. Ro., has had the fun of going out every night and the Classicist has had to stay home at nights, but the Pa. Ro. has to suffer intense pain and panic for a short period of time and the result of the examinations may not be satisfying. The Passionate Romantic loves to put on flashy clothes because they are in style. Before the Classicist will buy the modern fashions he will study the trends and try to learn how long the fashion will be fashionable. (How many of you Pa. Ro.'s still have Nehru jackets in your closets? Never heard of a Nehru jacket? Ask an old Passionate Romantic). The Pa. Ro. individual never considers his own personal pain when trying to do a good deed for somebody but later he feels abused or taken advantage of. A Classicist rarely does a good deed for anybody and late wonders if he missed an opportunity to help himself by helping somebody else.

Tell me, do you want a Passionate Romanticist for a President or do you want a Classicist? President John Kennedy was a Pa. Ro.. Back in 1961, in the month of October, we saw the perfect example of the Pa. Ro. at work. Russian boats were steaming toward Cuba when Kennedy decided to make them turn around in one of the most interesting, but dangerous confrontations of the Cold War. Mr. Kennedy strapped on his six shooters and faced down the nasty Soviets. The Soviets playing the part of the scroungy villains very well, smiled, kicked up dust with the tow of their boot and backed off. What if they hadn't? The Passionate Romantic was prepared to take that chance. . . unfortunately he was prepared to take a chance with your lives. But, hey, he won. He was a hero. When the Pa. Ro. wins, he wins big. When Jimmy Carter tried a Passionate Romantic rescue of the American captives in Iran he lost and lost big . . . an election. The move was ill planned, ill executed, but done with all the Passionate Romanticism that one needs to be a big hero . . . if he wins. If he loses, the Pa. Ro. looks like a fool. Abraham Lincoln was a true Classicist. He didn't say "free the slaves." He said we can't exist half slave and half free. We've got to be all or none. He fought the Civil War because if we hadn't, we could have been easy prey for the big European powers. If he had been a Passionate Romantic Civil Rights leader, the Proclamation of Emancipation would have come before the war, not nearly two years after the war started.

Now the reason I'm taking all of this time and energy to make this point clear (maybe I'm a Classicist?) is because I think the terms answer a great many questions as to why we love what we love in movies and in plays and why we hate what we hate. O.K., let's take one more movie and analyze its Passionate Romantic and Classical qualities: *Casablanca.*

It appears that Bogart is the classic Passionate Romantic in this movie. Is he? There is no doubt that this movie may be one of the five greatest films ever produced. Why? What about it still makes viewers sigh, cry and feel like a million dollars after it is all over? I think the use of Passionate Romanticism and Classicism is the reason. First, the movie is set in North Africa, a very romantic place filled with soldiers of fortune and swarthy characters, who deal in white slavery and other equally entertaining activities. And then again the movie is set in the middle of W W II which automatically gives a sense of romantic adventure to the whole picture. Then you have the most romantic screen hero to hit the movies since Valentino: Humphrey Bogart. It is impossible even to describe the impact Bogart had on audiences of his time and even audiences at this time. O. K., for those of you who don't know this film (breathes there a soul so dead) let me describe it for you. In the midst of W W II, Rick, an American ex-patriot, is living in Casablanca trying to get over a broken love affair. The whole idea of a man hiding away in a pest-hole in Africa. He's the Werther character feeling sorry for himself. But he's tough. He's tough in the super romantic style. He looks tough, he hits only once, and he's cool. Fonzie is a super romantic because he is cool, unruffled. So is Rick. Then, out of the blue, totally unexpected, his old flame (Ingrid Bergman) comes back into his life complete with a husband and asking favors. Here it is, the perfect Passionate Romantic situation, an open love wound. Rick, the guy who is so tough can't stand to hear a song that reminds him of his past love. As soon as Sam starts to play "As Time Goes By," Rick gets upset and makes him stop playing. He hurts inside his guts some place. His soul is tortured, and it is this tortured soul that is so attractive to women who saw the poor suffering hero and felt love and sympathy for him.

His ex asks the big favor. Her husband is an anti-Nazi trying to get out of Casablanca so that he can resume his political activities. Rick points out that the Nazis are all over this place and that he stays open because the Nazis think that he is apolitical. This is a very Classical argument. Rick hates the Nazis, but it is not in his interest to fight them. And besides, the French Prefect of Police, the most Classical character in the film, is always looking for an opportunity to gain favor with the Nazis without actually helping them, an closing Rick's place would be quite a feather in his cap. Rick is not going to risk everything he owns to help a woman who ran out on him and left him as a scarred individual forever. But his Passionate Romantic nature begins to take over and soon he is absolutely dedicated to winning his lover back. And, thanks to passion, she realizes that she is in love with him too. The plan is pretty simple: Rick will arrange to fly her husband out of Casablanca to a free country, and she will stay with him and together, as Passionate Romantics, they will live out their lives together. Simple, right? No. There are the Nazis to deal with. They are tough and they are Passionate Romantics too. They don't want people to be happy, but suffering is O.K.. In one of the brilliantly patriotic and passionate scenes of the movie, the Germans begin singing their national anthem. The French nationals in Casablanca begin to get angry, and soon they begin singing the French national anthem. Soon the scene becomes the passionate demonstration of patriotism that only a film like Casablanca can make work. And, of course, it all happens in Rick's Cafe so the Nazis begin to suspect that Rick may have sympathies that are not entirely healthy. As the movie goes on, Rick, who is falling more and more in love with his ex, begins to realize why she married her husband. Slowly Rick is being torn by that devil, reason. He begins to realize that if she stays with him in Casablanca that they both may die because life for him is not very safe. All of these rational thoughts are leading him away from the id of Passionate Romanticism and closer to the ego of Classical thought. At last the moment of truth occurs. Rick, in a violent struggle, frees his ex and her husband from the clutches of both the hated Nazis and the slimy Vichy French, and they all three find themselves standing in front of the waiting plane ready to carry off the husband and leave the wife, when all of a sudden the Passionate Romantic Rick reasons to his lover that she must not stay, that she must go with her husband because the husband needs her more than he does. It is an example of how classical reasoning can result in a passionate ending. She cries, he almost cries. She looks at her husband, he looks at her. She pleads silently for Rick to ask her to stay and he tells her to go. Incredible. She goes. The plane takes off. We see her face in the window, leaving her one chance for passionate happiness. She does her duty instead of following her passion. Rick does the same. Except in Rick's case the sacrifice is typical of the Passionate Romantic. And just when Rick thinks that he is now alone, the slimy Prefect of Police turns out to be not so slimy. He comes up to Rick, throws an arm around him and suggests both join up with the free French and try to beat the Nazis. Rick agrees. So it turns out the Classicist Perfect is actually a Passionate Romantic who is drawn to Rick because he is strong, passionate, and definitely a martyr. The movie ends with a sense of positive idealism as the two new friends walk into the fog.

So that's it for Passionate Romanticism and Classicism. If you're still confused think of these terms this way. Passionate Romantics are much like Liberals. They respond to techniques of social engineering that appeal to us emotionally. Classicists want to examine the logical and practical choices to social engineering. When President Clinton proclaimed that he felt "our pain" he proclaimed himself a Passionate Romantic. Can you guess what Rush Limbaugh is?

Tear-out Study Guide

1. Passionate Romantics think with their _____.

2. Passionate Romanticism started with a book called _____.

3. The author of the book was _____.

4. Gamblers are always good examples of _____.

5. The opposite of a Passionate Romantic is a _____.

6. President John F. Kennedy was an example of a _____.

7. *On The Waterfront* is an example of both _____and
_____.

8. Goethe became a Classicist because _____.

9. Hitler was a _____.

10. *Casablanca* is an example of _____.

Realism and
the Scientific Age

At last! We made it to 1800! The end of the 18th Century was a pretty boring time for theatre all over Europe. In the Germanic states Classicism was firmly entrenched. In France Napoleon's Passionate Romantic attempt to conquer the world made anything on stage seem boring. In Britain re-staging of Shakespeare, G. Rated copies of Restoration plays were being staged and Italy was spending its entertainment energy on operas and symphonies as was Austria. And all the while all our elements of theatre were stagnating. It was as if entertainment were waiting for something exciting, something revolutionary, something shocking to give theatre a jump start! And something was getting ready to do just that. Something was about to happen in the 18th Century that would give theatre such an incredible shot in the entertainment but that we're still feeling the effect.

Passionate Romanticism and Classicism battled into the 18th Century, and are battling even today for the minds and hearts of the people. Meanwhile, another form of theatre began developing during the 19th Century: Realism. It all had to do with the evolution of science. As the world began to learn about itself, it became scientifically curious about everything. In France, England, Germany, Russia, Norway, and Italy playwrights realized that people would really come to the theatre if they could discover something interesting and scientific about life. Hence the *well-made play* developed and it is still developing today. I think that the French were probably the most proficient in developing the *well-made play*. Eugene Scribe and Victorien Sardou produced play after play where the plot and story were almost identical to every other well-made play. Here is how the well-made play works. First, there is an incident: a murder, a theft, a marriage, a funeral, etc. During the incident a turn of events takes place. Let us say that a murder is committed and a police Lt. must solve the crime. Bit by bit he discovers clues until he comes to the conclusion and then, out of the blue, an important piece of information is discovered which changes everything and names the killer. Does this sound like *Colombo*? Exactly!

It is scientific in that it normally deals with a deductive plot where all the parts fit together like a jigsaw puzzle except that there is one piece that cannot be found until the end. It also deals with a prop which is always important to the plot. A missing gun turns up or a fan is discovered or a letter, hitherto unfound, is discovered. Now does this sound familiar to you? It ought to because it is basically the technique that almost all TV sit-drams use. Right, now you recognize it. You name the series and I'll show you how it works. Wait a minute, don't all shout at once. O.K., I hear *Quincy*. O.K., let's take *Quincy*. (For those of you who don't know that one, Dr. Quincy is a Medical Examiner in this series who solves crimes.) A murder is committed. Nobody can figure out what caused the death. Quincy goes in with all of his scientific knowledge and discovers that a certain kind of poison killed the victim. The police, using this information, arrest the man's business partner because a certain amount of this poison happens to be found on his shoes. The accused claims that he was only killing slugs in his backyard with the stuff, not his partner. Nevertheless, a jury of 12 good men find the guy guilty and sentence him to life in prison. But something bothers Quincy. He wants to investigate again. Nope. He can't. Case closed. He then violates the rules and makes more tests. He discovers a lump at the base of the victim's brain. Aha! It turns out that the lump was a tumor that killed the man, and the poison in his system actually came from a strawberry that the man had eaten in his partner's backyard the same day that the tumor took his life. The man is set free and justice is restored. There you have, the well-made play in all of its sitcom glory. Boring you say? Predictable, you say? Yes, both of these. Yet there are more well-made plays produced in the world every day then any other kind of entertainment. And in a way you like these simple minded plots with transparent characters. After all, you always know that justice will win out over evil. There is security in knowing that. And you also know that all of these sitcoms will be over in thirty or sixty minutes, so it is possible to leave your TV for many minutes at a time without missing too much. As long as you're there for the last six minutes, you'll learn everything there is to know about the whole show. The recognized leader in all of these sitdrams was the old Perry Mason show. Sixty minutes of action packed legal eagle stuff with always a dramatic witness and confession at the last moment. Perry always beat his arch nemesis, Mr. Burger, who always loses with no graciousness at all. Perry Mason went on for years winning and winning and winning. And when Perry Mason was tired of working in L.A. he went up to San Francisco and changed his name to Ironsides and kept right on winning and winning and winning. And, of course, there was the mandatory prop that always changed the plot, named the murderer, and got in some sneaky advertising for well known manufacturers. For example, in one episode of *Ironsides,* a rapist-murderer is loose in Golden Gate Park. Ironsides goes on TV with a panel of San Francisco officials in order to allow people to phone in and give information, if they have it, so they can publicly piece out the solution to the crimes. It turns out that the criminal has the habit of drinking coca-cola with peanuts in the bottle, a rather unusual technique. And then lo and behold, in the TV studio itself, there is a man sitting, drinking coca-cola with peanuts floating in it, just as Ironsides spots him. He is chased, brought down, and it urns out he is the murderer. And it all came to light because of a prop.

    All through the 1850's and 1860's this form of drama began drawing audiences. The shows were as good as the ones you see on TV today. The props kept popping up and the solutions to crimes, romances and very simple philosophical dramas kept the audiences guessing. But in the long run, these kinds of plays were not very satisfying. They're like peanuts, fun to eat but you can't exist on a diet of them. So somebody came up with an exciting alterative to the well-made play, which was even more based on scientific discovery than the previous plays were. It all really started in 1876 with the publication of Darwin's *Origin of the Species*. I know, you're saying, "What does a theory about evolution have to do with entertainment?" Good question. Here's the answer. After Darwin playwrights began to realize that there is a real animal nature about man, and it is just possible that not all men are as evolved as other men. It is just possible that some men are more ape-like in personality and thought than others. So, if you put two characters on stage that are in various states of evolution, it is possible that you can evolve some exciting relationships. And then there were those playwrights who realized that the human condition was really dependent on keeping alive the inferior among us, rather than allowing nature to take its course. Most civilized Europeans were not throwing their parents out on the block of ice to die of starvation when they got too old to feed themselves. Instead, they kept their parents around so they could abuse them in other ways. And, of course, there is the greatest playwright of this period, who was more interested in the hypocrisy of society then he was about the advancement of society. This playwright's name is Ibsen. Ibsen has a continuing effect on what we like in social theatre. He is one of greatest playwrights who ever lived, and one of the noisiest. Henrik Ibsen, a Norwegian playwright, came into his own during the 1880's. And the plays that really knocked audiences out were his one about the evils of society. In 1875 he wrote several plays which in the next decade brought light to several problems. The first was *Ghosts*. The play discusses the problem of venereal disease, and what happens when an innocent baby inherits the disease from his mother in the womb and grows up with the curse. Whose fault is this, screams the child who is afflicted. This is a problem we are still facing today. And then there was *Enemy of the People*. The play takes place in a small town in Norway. People come to this town in order to use the springs which are supposed to be very healthy for the bather. A Dr. Stockmann discovers that the springs are really very unsafe and that they have to be shut down. He claims that if the town doesn't close the baths, people will die. The town, however, doesn't want to lose the money that they get from tourists who come from all over the country to sit in the muddy, stinky and scientifically proven unhealthy baths. Stockmann says that you can't put money before the welfare of bathers. The town, however, really disagrees to the point that they make the good doctor an enemy and torture him. Does this sound familiar? Remember *Jaws*? Remember what the mayor says when he is given the information that there is a Great White Shark out there off the coast? He tells the scientist and the cop that they can't shut down the beach because the town makes its yearly living off the tourists who use the beach. Money over the welfare of the people who use the beach results in disaster. Ibsen wrote the same idea nearly a century before, and the point is still being made in movies. And what happens when you see an Ibsen movie idea about society? You get mad. You hate the dumb clucks who can't see the truth. The madder you get, the more interested you are in the outcome of the entertainment. Ibsen knew that and so did Spielberg when he made *Jaws*.

Ibsen took a real giant step out of the well-made play form of the years before: no more phony setups at the end, no surprise letters and missing pieces of evidence that just happen to show up to solve the problem of the play. And what is really important, Ibsen understood the nature of people and how to give them real shocks. In his play, *A Doll's House*, Ibsen really gives women's rights a boost up when at the end the wife of an over-bearing fool tells him to get another doll and walks out the door of her home so that she can grow into a woman. In *The Wild Duck*, a rumor about an extra-marital affair ruins the lives of an entire family. Who knows if the rumor is true? Certainly the people in the play don't really have proof for their actions, but thanks to a meddling idiot, a little girl is shot to death, a husband will live in a quilt forever, and a wife will never forgive her stupid husband for destroying the only thing that a poor family has, trust. Good soap operas look at Ibsen and steal his plots. Good movies look at Ibsen and steal his themes. Good movies look at Ibsen and steal his characters. You can always tell when you're seeing an Ibsen movie because nobody knows what is going on, but they proceed as if they do. The result is always chaos, but it is certainly interesting chaos.

At nearly the same time as Ibsen, a Frenchman named Andre Antoine was develop-ing another kind of theatre that was later called *naturalism*. Most experts in theatre scratch the naturalistic movement off as a waste of time, but it did produce one idea that we still use today. The naturalistic movement came out of that same era of scientific breakthroughs, only it was more interested in how things actually looked rather than how things could look. In other words, *naturalism* means that we observe an object of nature as it really looks. If the scene in the naturalistic play called for a piece of rotten meat, then the naturalists found a piece of rotten meat, crawling with maggots, attracting flies, and turning green, and stuck it right there up on the stage. The audience looked at it, held their nose, and left the theatre thinking that they had seen something shocking. The more the theatre advertised what the audience thought would be shocking, the more people came to the naturalistic theatre. Antoine, an employee for the Paris Gas Works (no joke) once put a horse on stage in his theatre. The horse got scared as soon as it saw all those people in the audience and immediately did what every scared horse would do. The actors spent most of their time trying not to "slip-up" on their lines. Even the horse began to lose his footing. The audience members got worried. The theatre was small and with a bit of bad luck the horse would be in the front row. But everybody made it through to the end of the play. And although it took a week to get the smell out of the theatre, everybody thought the play was a big success. Now what do we appreciate today that came from *naturalism*? Hang on, it isn't gonna be pretty. How many of you saw *The Thing*? I mean the latest thing that came out in 1982? Well, if you saw more of *The Thing* than you wanted, then most likely you got your fill of *naturalism. Naturalism* is committed to showing you everything no matter how boring or disgusting. When you hear the breaking of bones, the splitting of guts, the grinding of muscle, and then see some kind of a monster emerging from the very body of its host, then you are seeing naturalism. *Alien* gave you the treat of watching some ghastly monster emerging from the stomach of its human host. When it looks so real, it sometimes makes people throw up and become ill. Blood and guts films are so real sometimes that the management has to warn people that there are some scenes that will make you sick. The word "real" doesn't really fit. The word "natural" is what we're looking for. Do the makers of such films, which detail the horrible insides of intestines, really think that they are entertaining people? Yes, because the act of revulsion is somewhat entertaining. The makers of horror films and films where we see bullets go into bodies think that because we normally don't see such things, even though they do happen, that we will be curious enough to see what such gore looks like. They're right. Remember in the first chapter our description of the cars that slow down at an accident? People are curious, but remember this; once your curiosity has been satisfied, you rarely try to see these naturalistic pieces of gore again. Most of the people who see these things are kids. As we grow older and have acquired the experiences, the less we are motivated to recall them in the movie theatre.

Modern westerns really score in the areas of Realism and Naturalism. Take Clint Eastwood's *The Unforgiven*. If you look carefully at the movie you'll see the most amazing and disgusting things. You see outhouses, jail cells, greasy saloons and all of that stuff gives you the impression that the film is real and natural! Nothing is romantic and beautiful. The people in this film show you the disgusting and all too real and natural life in the old west. When people are shot they bleed all over the place. It's just as if the makers of the film wanted to convince you that you were really seeing a slice of life! Where you convinced? Did *Tombstone* convince you? *The Quick and the Dead* tried to show what it was like to watch a real slice of western Americana but then the film kept playing games with you. Instead of showing you a bullet entering a human body the film showed you a peep hole to look through a human body after it was shot. That's not real! But everything else in the movie was! So what we get when we put realism next to something which is not real is . . . confusion! The film wasn't too good but it was exciting! It was theatrical but it wasn't very dramatic. Understand? Being consistent is as important as being theatrical! Look at the movie, *Highlander*. The entertainment is based on your belief that the hero can't die. That isn't real. BUT his actions, his dialogue, and all of the sights and sounds around him are real! Scotland is real! New York is real! So what do you make of all of this? Well, first if you buy into the supernatural then the supernatural becomes real! If you buy into the idea that it is natural for a supernatural human to die and come back to life then wounds that heal up instantly, organs which were smashed by a bullet one moment heal up in another then we are seeing realism when the Highlander does all of these fantastic things! However, when you watch a football game you're seeing Naturalism! You watch the huddle, you watch the incomplete pass, you watch the TV timeouts, and you watch the halftime. You watch everything for three hours because that's how long the game takes. . . got it? Nothing has been selected out of the game and shown to you. Now, if later you go home and watch the sports report at the end of the news and the report only shows you the three scoring plays of the game . . . that's Realism!

It seems that society wants to see Realism more and more. Maybe our minds are a little too narrow to imagine what is not presented to us. In Shakespeare's day the audience had to do a lot of imagining. But after Darwin our society evolved into a very real world. . . a world that doesn't allow us to play around with the truth! So how does the *Lion King* fit into this? Can lions talk? Can lions think? Can lions extrapolate (look it up in the dictionary!)? Of course not. But if you believe that lions can do all of those things then they can. And of course you're watching a cartoon. . . an animation! Animation isn't real unless you *suspend* your disbelief and accept drawings as real people. Then what happens when we see a film like *Who Killed Roger Rabbit?* Now we've got live people playing with cartoons! Oh boy. This is a big problem. But there is also a pretty good answer to these last questions. And the answers are going to come in the next chapter. Did you look up "extrapolate"? Don't be lazy. Do it or you won't understand what's going on in Chapter Ten.

CHAPTER NINE

Tear-out Study Guide

1. Realism developed as a result of the evolution of _____.

2. The French were probably the most proficient at writing the _____play.

3. Henrik Ibsen wrote a play called _____ which discussed the subject of venereal disease.

4. The play, *A Doll's House* gives a boost to _____ rights

5. Andre Antoine developed a kind of theatre that became known as _____.

6. Modern westerns really score in the areas of _____ and _____.

7. The TV series, *Columbo* is an example of _____.

8. A prop is always important to the plot of the _____.

9. In *Enemy of the People* the springs are _____.

10. When you sit down in front of the TV and watch a football game which is unedited you are watching an example of _____.

The Certifiable Movement

As soon as God and God's plan for the universe came into question artistic chaos exploded on the theatre scene. It wasn't a situation of the average person on the street suddenly leaping up and saying, "Hey! Maybe there's no God!" Not anything like it. But it did confirm what a lot of heavy thinkers had considered going all the way back to the ancient Greeks. "Maybe this whole religion thing is far more complex and unknowable than the priests have led us to believe!" Exactly! One of those individuals who was pretty confused and liked being confused was a Frenchman named, Alfred Jarry. Most people thought Jarry was crazy. But he was rich and that only made him eccentric. He lived in Paris in the 1890s and spoke to a generation of people who were enjoying arguably, the greatest explosion of art and appreciation for art in the history of the western world!

In 1870 France had lost the Franco-Prussian War which allowed the Germanic states to form a union which was called Germany. France, rightly so, said that the unification of those war-like states would plunge Europe into war. Well, not a lot of people believed that which just goes to show you how stupid people can be! But for the next 44 years Europe would enjoy a kind of peace which would allow the countries to spend lots of money on art and especially theatre. Going to the theatre in those days was much like going to the movies today. There was a good chance you would see a pile of garbage but there was also a slim chance that you would see something wonderful and extraordinary. Mind bending! You might see something that would allow your mind to extrapolate and transcend time and space and carry you off to some hitherto unexplored territory . . . kind of like *Star Trek* or maybe Peewee Herman. And of course it was all Darwin's discoveries which were prompting all of this stuff! Arthur Conon Doyle was experimenting with a scientific detective called Sherlock Holms! We were on the verge of making motion pictures! We even started considering the possibility of flying to the moon thanks to Jules Verne! Exciting stuff. And most of this marriage between art and science was happening in Paris! And Jarry was enjoying it more than anybody else. In fact . . . he was causing a lot of the entertainment that made Paris such a fun place. Jarry was nuts. He was totally certifiable and should have been committed to a hospital for his own good. But he was too rich (inherited money) to be handled. He simply bought off any problems that occurred because of his strange habits.

Let us understand right now that nobody can really discuss Jarry. Why? Because Jarry is beyond real description for most normal people. He was an explosion of originality. He was a nightmare. He was a ferris wheel ride gone out of control. He was both repulsive and immediately attractive. He was so insane that some people think that he actually turned the bend to sanity while everybody else must be insane by comparison. What he discovered about art and theatre has had such a smashing impression on us that most of us don't realize how early in life we are affected by Jarry, and how deeply he controls the nature of our lives. Now I know that those are rather heavy descriptions of a guy who only lived for about twenty-five years and actually only produced a few difficult-to-understand plays, but I'm not talking about his contributions to *Drama*. I'm talking about what he did for *Theatre*. Who was Jarry? Some people say that the grandest time to live in the grandest city ever was the 1890's in the city of Paris. It was a magnificent time. War, recession, depression, and starvation took a backseat to dancing, loving, art, and philosophy. What a time to live! In this sheltered and exciting little harbor of sanity came the grand lunatic, Alfred Jarry. I guess he was crazy if we judge the standards of sanity by a majority vote; he certainly didn't vote with the majority. Jarry had money, his family had position, and he had a great deal of free time. As a child he drove his teachers crazy. He didn't want a traditional education. He wanted an education that would prepare him for the consciousness of being. He wanted to learn why the looking glass always made you look fat (or does it make you look thin?) He wanted to know what happened if you held two looking glasses up to each other and then crawled into one of the mirrors, or into both of the mirrors. Jarry wanted to know what happened to the sound after he sang. He wanted to know where the sound went, and why did it go there and did it ever come back? Jarry wanted to know if a smile took longer to form than a frown and, if so, why didn't people smile more? He wanted to know if puppets ever took on the souls of their puppeteers. Jarry wanted to know if there was a door to another dimension of life, which turned people invisible in the third dimensional world. He asked these questions of his teachers and I think he got beatings for an answer. He was a lonely little boy who probably played by himself, had friendly ghosts who shared his inner thoughts and playful spirits who urged him on to mischief. When he finally reached what most of his generation would call adulthood, he was still a little boy. He came to Paris in the 1890's and became a personality. Some called him an eccentric. Some called him a simple minded lunatic. Many invited him to speak to social groups, because he was witty and could make fun of any social convention you could name. At great expense he bought Jesse James' guns and strapped them around his body as he walked down the streets of Paris. He wore a long black robe, sported a beard with cut-out patches in it, and spoke in a long slow drawl that made his speech sound as if it were recorded at 75 rpms and played back at 33 1/3 rpms. He bought an apartment house in Paris where he lived in comfort. One of his close friends, Toulouse-Lautrec, wanted to move in. So Jarry took one of the apartments and divided it in half so that people coming into Lautrec's apartment would have to bend over and be conspicuous. He felt that Lautrec had to spend most of his time being conspicuous in a giant world, but he ought to have the pleasure of being normal in his own home. Jarry befriended a struggling Picasso and a developing Beardsly. He loved wild and talented people, because he felt that he was a wild and talented man. Jarry set a standard for entertaining lunacy that has made modern actors stars. Robin Williams, Jonathan Winters, Steve Martin, and even Woody Allen have borrowed and used Jarry's strange and wonderful views of the world. Jim Carrey and Jeff Daniels have discovered Artaud in *Dumb and Dumber.*

In 1896 Jarry produced a play that turned the world of entertainment upsidedown: *Ubu Roi*, Ubu the King. The play tried, successfully tried, to destroy all the existing theatre values. It was outrageous, destructive, and so audacious that it was closed down immediately for public indecency. We think Jarry based the play on an old science teacher he once had, who was particularly nasty to him. The play occurs in Poland where a Macbethian character tries to gain power exactly as the Shakespearean Macbeth had gained power; he murdered, he cheated, and he lied. In the process of the play Macbeth, I mean Ubu, eventually scoops out the brains of his subjects, yet they can all walk around as before, only they have no will but Ubu's. One might think that high school science student Jarry objected to the attempts of his teacher to make him conform to the standard rules. No doubt Jarry thought they were trying to steal his individuality. So now in *Ubu Roi* he looks backwards, forwards, and at the present (all at the same time) as he points out how silly middle-class values are. Never before had anybody dreamed of putting anything like this on the stage. During one of the scenes the Polish and Russian armies meet each other, only they are basically just little cartoon characters.

In December of 1896 at the Theatre Le l'Oeuvre in Paris (you mean you never heard of it?) Jarry announced to the middle-class folks of Paris that a new and wild concept in theatre staging was going to be presented. When the audience came into the theatre, they saw Jarry himself up on stage playing cards. He just sat there looking at his cards and ignoring the audience. The lights dimmed and Jarry looked out at the audience and the curtain went up. Jarry waddled down to the footlights, said in the slowed down speech, "Shi-i-i-i-i-i-it." (Some say another actor said it, but I'm betting it was Jarry). The audience was shocked! Nobody had ever said a word like that to a French audience, whether they deserved it or not. Jarry did. The journalists covering the fantastic opening scribbled quickly. Jarry then told the audience that the play was "set in Poland, that is to say it is set nowhere." As far as we know, that was the first Polish joke ever given on stage. The play also ended with a Polish joke, "After all, if there weren't a Poland, there would be no Poles." The French did not laugh during the show (maybe some of them had seen Macbeth before and were bored). The French audience reacted as if they had been slapped in the face. They didn't know what to make of all of this. They thought the play was vulgar, shocking, and insulting. What Jarry wanted them to think was that the play was vulgar, shocking, and insulting. It was a success (only Jarry and his cast thought so, however). The world was not ready for Jarry. He was a man so far ahead of his time that there are those today who don't understand him. They don't understand why his actors acted like puppets, or why they had crocodile heads, or why there was so much cruelty in the play. Lenny Bruce would have understood. Richard Pryor would have understood. And most of all, Will Rogers would have and did understand. There is a movie called *Tron*, an adventure in a computer which easily could have been conceived and written by Jarry. Except Jarry would never have allowed it to be produced, unless people would be grossly insulted by it. But then again Fox's *House of Buggin'* is Jarry as well!

So what after all was Jarry trying to do and why? Was he just a certifiable character who needed to spend time in a lunatic asylum? Maybe! But that is not all he was. Jarry unlocked the key to our imaginations. He made us break our visionary molds and furthermore, he would let us put together any other molds. He wanted us to see life from a million points of view with none of them being right or wrong. Jarry might have even doubted that we even existed at all. He was sure that life had to be entertaining, not restricted. Out of Jarry we get Benny Hill, Monty Python Company, Ernie Kovacs (if you don't know who Ernie Kovacs was, then go directly to jail and do not pass Go, you're out of the game). Jarry refused to allow boredom to dominate his life. Hell, he refused to let boredom enter his life! He gave us a crazy world to laugh at and enjoy. He gave us *Saturday Night Live* the way the original *Saturday Night Live* gang saw life. And here it comes gang: he gave us the word *absurd* (well, he didn't say that but this is what he meant, I think?). Absurd, as in meaningless, as in don't give a damn, as in we are all born to die so why not have as much fun along the way as possible. The next time you get a chance, study Rocky and Bullwinkle of the old *Rocky Show*. The show is silly, satirical, and absolutely fun. Jarry would have said, "This is finally what I'm after." Now I know that Rocky is just a cartoon. Yes, I know that it is designed for kids. Yes, I know that the show just wastes good air time, but that is the whole point. You enjoy it, you relax with it, and you have no bad aftertaste. You don't have to think or draw any political and social conclusions. You can just love it without it loving you back. Remember our definition of Theatre: laughter. The ability not only to laugh at somebody else, but to be able to laugh at yourself. When you stop taking yourself so seriously, then you rarely get mad, insulted upset, or "uptight." What do you get? Peace of mind. Now, does that sound so crazy? Is that certifiable? Remember sanity is only a majority vote and maybe Jarry should have gotten more votes. Or perhaps his vote was really the only one that counted!

We have to leave Jarry, although it would be lots of fun to explore him a great deal, because we really need to get to the next theatre movement. And even though we're going to be talking about somebody else, we're really never going to leave Jarry. You'll see what I mean. In the same year that Jarry's *Ubu Roi* was produced, a fellow named Antonin Artaud was born. He grew up loving Jarry, and in 1938 he opened the Jarry Theatre. Artaud loved Jarry's theory of life and theatre so much that he tried to imitate him in every way (it should be noted that Jarry drank himself to death at a very early age and Artaud tried to do the same thing with drugs). Only Artaud decided, eventually, to take

Jarry's theories one step further. In the late 1930's he invented Theatre of Cruelty. What is this? *The Rocky Horror Picture Show*, *The Thing*, and *Rocky I, II, III* are examples of Artaud's theatre. Artaud felt that life had to get down to the essential meaning. Artaud felt that passion, pure and simple, was the governing force behind all human communication. Words, he said, were useless (Jarry felt the same way and made fun of the way words were used to lie and cheat in big business, the Church, and in the bedroom). Artaud said that if you look at nature, it will tell you all you have to know about the rhythm of life. Passion in every move, life and death at every turn, complete devotion to movement. Take a look at *Rocky III*. When Rocky is told that he needs to recapture the "eye of the tiger," he means that Rocky has to get hungry. Rocky has to stop thinking and start feeling. Rocky has to stop allowing civilization to make his decision for him. He has to find his primordial roots and allow his basic creation to dominate his life. When he does that he doesn't need words, he just needs commitment. And most of us have to agree the Rocky films have a certain beauty that Artaud would call "the return to naked passion."

The Thing is Artaud because it communicates through blind rage and anger. Artaud says that a grunt tells us more about feelings than an essay. *The Thing* shows us disgusting *spectacle*, incredible *violence*, and most of all the words are only secondary to the natural fear that is inspired by being close to something that is so alien that it can't communicate in any other way except death. For Artaud, death is the ultimate answer to life. It solves all our problems, and it leaves us complete. Nothing in nature lives forever. All of it changes and all of us change. Death for Artaud is only the last change in our lives, nothing more. In *The Thing* (1982 version) it is made crystal clear that everybody will die. In the end the Thing is no different than the earthlings, it dies, they die. They are equal and alike in death.

The Rocky Horror Picture Show is also Artaud in that the physical commitment of the play makes us laugh and also makes us a trifle revolted. We are shocked by the *bizarre*. Artaud demands that you be shocked in his theatre. There is much passion in the picture, especially in the music which attacks our emotions through its rhythms. The plot is simple minded but the characters are diseases! Artaud would have loved them. The scenes of seduction are animal-like, which turns and shocks the audience. And the most important characteristic is the dialogue. The dialogue is silly, and stupid, and mostly meaningless, which is exactly how Artaud feels about words in the first place. All of the above motion pictures are super examples of Artaud's theories, but there is one movie that is the absolute definitive example of Antonin Artaud. It is a movie called *The Naked Prey*.

If you have not seen Cornell Wilde's *The Naked Prey*, then put it down on your list of "must see movies when they come to TV." The picture is a monument to the Theatre of Cruelty. The story takes place in Africa around the turn of the century. A safari is making its way through the jungle, on a hunting expedition. The clients are selfish overbearing fools. The leader of the safari obviously hates them. Suddenly a fierce tribe of warriors surrounds the safari. The leader of the safari asks in the native tongue what they want. They tell him that they want gifts. During all of this there are no subtitles, but it is obvious through the passion of the sounds what is going on. Naturally, the clients bully the natives and refuse the traditional gifts. The leader of the safari tells them that they are crazy. But, of course, they ignore his good advice. Trouble flares up and before you know it, a thousand warriors chase the safari members down and kill most of them. A few of them, including the clients and the leader of the safari, are taken prisoner by the natives. The prisoners are then tortured and killed in the most cruel and ingenious ways. Everybody dies except the leader of the safari. He is to participate in a ritual murder which gives him a chance to run for his life. The only catch is this: he must be stripped naked like an animal. The rest of the movie tells the story of the manhunt. The sounds you hear are jungle sounds, and the native language which nobody understands intellectually but everybody understands through the emotions. The whole movie is made up of scenes of African violence, but there is an absolute dedication to beauty by the makers of the film. The soul speaks in this film, not the tongue. Artaud would have loved it. Primordial passion in all of its fierce glory. You leave the movie just as if you experienced the events yourself.

Quest for Fire tries to do the same thing. Many of you loved the film because the communication was purely on a physical level. The intellect never got in the way of the prime reason for seeing the film: man in his most natural state. The sound track of the film is basic and simple. It is rhythm. Artaud loved music, which was simply a drum beat, a hollow native sound without pretensions and melody. The savage rhythm of the music must be the same rhythm of the heartbeat. And *The Mask* achieves the same thing. Artaud's life could make an interesting movie all by itself. First he started out as a "pretty boy" movie actor. Then he realized that his physical beauty got in the way of his communication with people so he destroyed that beauty with drugs and hard living. Second, he formulated most of his ideas about theatre while going insane. He traveled to Mexico and lived with the Yaquis. He smoked drugs and injected drugs. then he came back to Europe where he was confined to an insane asylum in Ireland and given electro-shock treatment. He escaped from the asylum and then he was brought back. Finally, after WWII, his friend, Eugene Ionesco, got him out of jail, and he lived the rest of his life in semi-sanity, often lapsing into periods of complete incomprehensibility. Poor Artaud! His genius was so pure that it couldn't even be understood by his closest friends. He was much like a conduit with too big a change . . . it blew him away. But Lord, what incredibly complicated and exciting ashes. Artaud was pure *Theatre*.

In the very same way, the work of Mel Brooks leans toward Artaud. Brooks, of course, is definitely directed by Jarry, but now and then there occurs a strange and wonderful characteristic in Brooks' films, which tends to make me wonder if Mr. Brooks would make a serious film in the Artaud fashion, might we not see a brilliant piece of work? Let us take Brooks' *The Producers*. First, it is a very funny film because the ideas are funny and the situations are funny and most of all it is all presented by several funny actors. But if you look closely at the film, you will notice that beneath the comedy, there is a sense of loneliness and vulnerability which leads us to extreme pain. There is a frustration in this film which gets straight to the passion of the film. Two swindlers try to produce a play, which will lose money because all the plays that one of the swindlers has produced have lost money. Now when they need a big loser and do everything rationally to create a big loser so that they can keep the money they raised for the play, it turns out to be a winner. The terrible irony of the film deals with the simple subject of rational behavior. All of these years one of them had been trying every way he knew to make money, and when he put all of that losing experience to work for him, it turned out disastrous. What this means is that knowledge is meaningless! Experience doesn't count for anything! Artaud would have agreed himself!

Amusement parks have that Theatre of Cruelty feeling. The idea is to climb into one of those fast flying, terrifyingly entertaining thrill rides at Great America or Six Flags West and scare yourself silly. Lots of fun for a generation that is constantly looking for the bigger and better thrill!

Virtual reality games are also grounded in Artaud. Participation in the basic thrill that either frightens you or satisfy you. Hooking yourself up to machine that will give you the feeling of flying in a jet plane even though you never leave your chair is the ultimate thrill since it gives you all of the sense of danger without any of the reality of it.

When we go to the movies nowadays there's a pretty good chance that the film will in some way reflect one of Jarry's or Artaud's theories about theatre. Your generation is so dedicated to finding the intense thrill that movie makers will do just about anything to convince you that their products will send you into that crazy state of disbelief known as "mindlessness"! Pure theatre without the interferences of drama is the passionate goal of the certifiable theatre movement.

CHAPTER TEN

Tear-out Study Guide

1. Alfred Jarry was a _____who lived in Paris during the 1890s.

2. *Ubu Roi* was written by _____.

3. *The Naked Prey* is an example of _____.

4. Antonin's ideas about passion in theatre created the "Theatre of _____."

5. In a strange way Mel Brooks leans towards _____.

6. _____ got Artaud out of jail after WWII.

7. Artaud loved Jarry's _____ and _____.

8. Artaud went to Mexico to study the _____.

9. *Ubu Roi* takes Shakespeare's play _____ and distorts it.

10. Amusement parks have that _____ of _____ feeling.

The Cloud and Beyond

The most important single event that changed the entire history of the world occurred in 1945: the A Bomb. When we dropped it on Japan, we changed history forever. We opened the door to self-destruction and it has never been closed since. When that terrible mushroom cloud formed over what had been living people, we lost something that we have never regained, our sanity. From that time on, we have lived under that cloud waiting for the absolute truth to occur. And in a very real way it is all entertaining to us. Somehow the atomic tension that we live under every day of our lives since 1945 until 1994 caused us to *anticipate* the worst and so far, thank God, we are still anticipating. The A Bomb didn't just change us, it has destroyed us just as surely as if the damn thing had been dropped. It has made us worry, create great stockpiles of A Bombs, and launch satellites around the globe with the idea of placing A Bombs in orbit! And what happened to our condition is seen directly through theatre as it has developed since 1945. Remember that work *absurd*? Well now we can use it freely because we are definitely all living under mad, insane, and completely absurd conditions. Do you know that we have a bomb so powerful that we are afraid to test it? We have the cobalt bomb that we think could actually crack the earth's core if exploded. We think it might be able to move us out of orbit with that thing. And if we moved out of orbit, we would affect our solar system which would affect our galaxy which in turn would affect our universe? Now if that is not crazy and insane and absurd, then we gotta have another vote! Out of all of this came the great and very amusing *Absurdists*. Leader of the pack was a guy named Ionesco, whom we mentioned was a friend of Artaud's. Ionesco worshipped Jarry and Artaud. He hated what the world had done to itself. And I think he hated God for creating us so that we can die. Ionesco didn't like death and he certainly didn't like the idea of waiting for salvation. Ionesco wanted it all now, but there is nothing to want so life is silly and useless and the sooner we forget it the better. Ionesco and Woody Allen are very similar in their development of lonely people who have little to live for because they are so pitifully stupid. Woody's *Love and Death, Annie Hall, Take the Money and Run* and his countless other film take a wild and completely unconventional look at life.

Woody studies the pit in great detail. What you think Woody will say, he won't and what you never would have thought he would say, he says so easily and offhandedly that you are taken by mental surprise and you laugh. The *absurdists* do exactly the same thing. They do it over and over and over because they want you to know that life is worthless. So go ahead and laugh at it. Woody doesn't think life is worthless. On the contrary, he feels life is so important that he overemphasizes the necessities of life to a point that he becomes ridiculous. He bends the absurdist ideas so far back they almost break but don't. We laugh at the way he bends them, and sometimes we are a little sad when he can't straighten them out again.

The absurdists live while expecting death at any time. They produce plays and films that tell us that death is just around the corner. So why not laugh at all since you are powerless to stop it. The most important absurdist to come out of Europe is not the heavyweight playwrights, such as Ionesco and Beckett, but Peter Sellers. He contributed a film to us just before he died that put him at the top of the list of all the absurdists who ever lived. Not only did he make the film a statement for all of us to appreciate, but he made it for all of those children in the next generations who will look back at our society and say, "Aha, I understand what our ancestors were all about." The film is called *Being There*. It is monumental. It is the greatest piece of absurd theatre and the greatest denial of absurd theatre that was made in our generation. Looks like I'm contradicting myself, right? No. It does serve two purposes and after our discussion I think you'll see my point. For those of you who never saw the film (for which I am very sorry for you), I'll review it. Somewhere in Washington, D.C., lives a strange little man who takes care of flowers. The house is going to be taken away from him and he is going to be turned out. He has never been out. As far as he knows, he knows nothing of the outside world. For all intents and purposes he is insane. He never seems to understand threats of violence, and his incredible simplicity is never interpreted as childlike by anybody, because nobody would ever believe that he could be so childlike. Through absurd circumstances he becomes the advisor and friend to people in the highest political offices in the country. He goes on TV as an influential advisor to the President of the United States, where he talks about gardening, but everybody thinks that he was talking about the "ship of state." People hear what he says in his simple little way and seem to find dramatic ramifications. We laugh at all of this, because we think the people are so silly for listening to a half wit. Bit by bit this moron gets power, only he doesn't know he's getting power. And finally near the end of the film, important people are talking about running him for President. The audience is in hysterics thinking that the people, who want to elect this stupid little man to the highest office, must be even more idiotic than the gardener. And then at the very end of the film there is a funeral for the gardener's closest friend (although the gardener never really treated him with an special love). And at the funeral, where the gardener's name is being forwarded for the highest office in the land, we see the gardener walking on water. In one blockbuster scene we see the entire film changed, reversed, and thrown back shockingly into our faces.We thought the gardener was an idiot because he said things like "all the garden needs is a little water, some sunlight, and love" when somebody asked him how to cure the ills of the nation. Now we realize that his innocent view toward life was inherent in Godliness. No idiot here, just virgin beauty. Absurd, of course, because nobody recognizes the Almighty when He actually comes to us. Not absurd because the absurdists saw no hope for mankind at all, but this movie tells us that as long as God is tending the Garden, there is hope for us all.

It seems interesting to me that Peter Sellers' last film was one that celebrated life in a beautiful and sensitive way. A person could find no better way to leave one's career for posterity. In one film Sellers isolated his comedy technique, his humanity, and his artistic skill. In one film he wrapped up twenty-five years of comedy successes and he surpassed all of his previous films. And in one film he insulted Mr. Death to his face.

In the 1960s a particular playwright named Harold Pinter created a style of play which combined elements of Jarry, Artaud, Ionesco, and blended them all together into his own form, which has done more to create interest in theatre than any other contemporary writer. Harold Pinter developed the technique of the unsaid. His plays reflect violence, yet rarely does anybody get hurt in his plays. They reflect his society, yet is always difficult to determine exactly what part of his society he is attacking or praising. They reflect the familiar characters who surround our lives, yet his characters are almost impossible to identify out of plays. In short, Pinter is a master of making the insignificant seem grotesque. He takes everyday occurrences and makes them seem important. A simple "hello" can all of a sudden, in a Pinter play, seem to be a dangerous statement. In a Pinter play the characters infer that something is going on, but never really come out and say it. The tantalizing ideas that are almost said drive the audience crazy. In Pinter's *The Birthday Party* it seems that a rather nasty tongued fellow named Stanley is hiding out in a boarding house at a seaside resort. Two other fellows come to get him and they do. That's it. The whole plot is as simple as it can be, but oh what Pinter does with that simple plot. He suggests that two guys who come to get the third are gangsters. He suggests that the two know something about the third which is dangerous and terrible. He suggests that the two actually destroy the third with words. When the play is over, you think you have had a rather exciting experience, but it is difficult to describe what actually happened. Harold Pinter's greatest film is *The French Lt.'s Woman,* which won him critical praise. In this film he takes a set of actors, a man and a woman, and he traces their brief relationship as they play both dramatic characters in a period film and themselves as they rehearse the film within the film. Pinter is so skillful at revealing the personalities of the characters that sometimes we don't even know which of the relationships is the real relationship for the good of the film. Or perhaps both relationships are equally as important, or perhaps that neither of them are real. Mr. Pinter is an exciting playwright because his Drama is sometimes more theatrical than the elements of Theatre designed to help the Drama.

And this now finally brings us to the present. The present is easy now that we have examined the past. Today there is one entertainer that stands head and shoulders above the rest (yes, he has clean hair too): Steven Spielberg. He started out at 20 by directing

Marcus Welby television episodes and now he is the greatest storyteller in films in the history of the business, and that includes John Ford, John Huston, and the rest. Spielberg is a rare individual. He knows how to take an idea, expand it so that it is greater than itself, present it to an audience in a near flawless manner, and make that audience love every second of the entertainment. He is the true maker of films for all ages. His best film, *E.T.,* is a combination of everything good in Drama and in Theatre. It is a masterpiece. Mr. Spielberg can take a bit of light, focus it at the right time at the right place, and suddenly magic happens. At the same time, he can take a word, a word so simple and basic, and turn it into a beautiful and sensitive expression of humanity. He can take the violent actions of a Great White Shark and make them seem almost human in their motivation. All in all Spielberg has it all. He is the perfect combination of intelligence, creativity, and theatrical skill. He draws upon everything in the past to recreate the present. His films have the morality of a Greek play. They are blatantly violent as the most violent Roman theatre. His use of the camera is as poetic as Shakespeare's words. His sensitivity to passion makes him a Passionate Romantic, but his sure sense of right and wrong makes him a Classicist. His statement about society and the human condition is worthy of Ibsen, and his sense of fantasy would make Jarry giggle. His use of alien forms, which visit this planet, almost gives us a sense of absurdism, but like *Being There,* Spielberg always lets us know that there is help out there for us.

Spielberg's entertainment empire has grown so big that he is an entertainment rule maker himself. Whatever he produces becomes a standard . . . only in America!

Well, it looks as if we won't blow each other off the planet! The A Bombs are locked up and diffused, we won't have to drag out any dooms day weapons and all we seem to be interested in nowadays is having fun. Entertainment will supply the fun! Take a look at the new virtual reality movies that are making the rounds of theaters. Everybody gets a chance to sit in the theater and watch a film in which the audience can control the action! Right! You get a remote control and if enough of you want to send the film into a different direction, then you press the button and you make the movie change! Incredible.

Soon, you'll be able to feel movies because your chairs will move with the action. You'll be able to smell bacon cooking over an open camp fire. Or before the sexy lady enters the screen, you'll smell her perfume. Right now you can go to Luxor in Las Vegas and take a virtual reality ride that will shock you and rock you! When the threat of WWIII vanished, so did the fear and anticipation of the event. Instead we're afraid of ozone holes, deadly viruses, and our neighbors!

Sure, since worldwide violence doesn't scare us any more we've decided to scare ourselves with gang violence and its ultimate promise of chaos and death. We worry about crime in the streets getting more prevalent. We worry about drugs, consumer rip-offs and international industrial spying. See? The beat always goes on and the opportunities to amaze and delight you are always there too. Since "theatre" really depends on shocking your emotions, it stands to reason that technology and its evolution will continue to do so. 70 mm film is the heart of virtual reality sensation and there's no question that we've only scratched the surface of that kind of involvement.

Well, here we are folks. We tore through three thousand years of theatre in just a few pages of work. What have we accomplished? What have we discovered? What do we understand about entertainment that we didn't know before? Plenty. First, we started out with a definition of two words, *Drama* and *Theatre*. We learned that *Drama* is what you say and *Theatre* is how you say it. And we discovered that how you say something can be very complex. The more theatrical tricks that are used to say something, the more difficult it can become to understand what is being said. Yet, if no theatre is used, then what is said can become very boring. Then we traveled through history to observe what has passed for theatre and drama in several cultures. We learned that almost every country we visited had something of importance to tell us about entertainment. Building blocks. If we put them together carefully, we can see exactly what has caused us to enjoy the present entertainment forms. Some of us love violent films on the Roman scale. Some of us like the Passionate Romantic plays that make our hair rise on the back of our necks. Many of us love the power and strength of Shakespearean plots. And then again, social criticism plays and films capture the imagination of millions. Almost all of us love a good laugh at the expense of others, and so Jarry gets on the entertainment train with us. But no matter what we have discovered, there is still one conclusion that I would like to leave with you. Entertainment deals with the human soul. The human soul can be touched by everything; it is a slate on which theatre and drama are always leaving their marks. How you are marked is up to you. You can let naturalistic violence scar you, if you like, through repeated exposure. You can wallow in the well-made play TV sitcoms which will amuse you. And you can bore yourself with meaningless, artless, pseudo-adventure films which have predictable conclusions and unsuitable philosophies. Or you can uplift your soul. You can expose it to the finest collaboration of mind and emotion that exists in entertainment today. You can tantalize your spirit with ideas that demand you reach deep inside of yourself, searching for the meaning of your existence on this planet. You can use the basic principles of theatre and drama to introduce yourself to the divine and the sublime. Action and idea simply mean knowledge, knowledge of yourself in every way. Knowledge of what has had meaning for us in the past, what has meaning for us in the present, and what we hope will have meaning for us tomorrow. Look hard, and then let your emotions blend with your intellect and choose your path. I have faith that you will march in the right direction.